FAITH BY FIRE

Finding God on His Terms

By
Nelson Thomas

Laurie,

There are no coincidences in this life. May God bless & keep you.

Contents

Faith by Fire

𝐫

Initially, this book was designed as an outreach to those who had experienced suicide within their family. "What's Left of a Son," the initial title, detailed the five years of devastation and turmoil that followed my mother, Marsha Lynn Thomas, taking her own life. While my intentions were good, the book left only a sense of loss and nothing gained. Situations arose after I had completed the first version which turned my world upside down all over again. These situations increased to a point in which I nearly became a casualty of suicide myself. But that's when the most important experience of my life took place; I found God and His purpose for my life. The impact of that revolution changed me forever. My pain ... gone. My fear of the future ... vanished. In God, I not only found the peace which passes all understanding but also His purpose for my life.

From there, I became His instrument, and my life was transformed from one full of chaos to that which wanted to save others from theirs. A career's worth of dedication to saving lives became a heartfelt, life-altering quest to save souls.

Refreshed and fully aware of its purpose, I re-engaged on writing a book detailing my journey through life's insanity to ultimately find God. This book addresses major issues such as suicide, chemical addiction and abuse, death of a friend and coworker, personal insanity, depression, anxiety, and my own close call with suicide. But on the flip side, it also details my misunderstandings of God and how He eventually drove me to my passion of inspiring others to hang on through life's unmistakable turmoil.

Nelson Thomas

In loving Memory of
Marsha Lynn Thomas

&
Derek Vincent Kozorosky

1

Growing Up Different

G rowing up, I was always different than most guys my age. While everyone else was worried about sports and fast cars, I was more into my writings and music. I was a deep thinker with an imagination only I could understand. I cared a lot more about the purpose of life and the coming of death; maybe a little too much. Perhaps I watched "Dead Poets Society" one too many times with the result that I became overly enamored with "seizing the day" and "sucking the marrow out of life." Later, I became even more intrigued with the depth that life can bring. When everyone else was only concerned with the black and white, I closely examined the perplexing gray area. At times I wondered if there was something wrong with me, yet later I realized that I just cared until it hurt.

One thing I didn't like or understand about myself was that I always thought, if not fantasized, about suicide. I never understood why, but it had always been something I thought about, not on a daily basis, but more often than most. Ever since I was a mid-teen it haunted me. It wasn't that I wanted to commit suicide; I can't imagine what my reason would be. But the thought was always there for reasons I couldn't understand.

The only reason I could consider was the excessive amount of suicides which happened around me to people I knew either directly or indirectly. From sports heroes, to musicians, friends, or extended family members, suicide just seemed to be one of those things that I heard of way too often.

One thing to note is that I was extremely close to my mother in my younger years. While my brother went on fishing trips with my dad, I would stay at home with my mother. I can't say that I disliked this situation much, being that I remained a well-dressed high schooler due to our numerous shopping excursions. This amount of time together allowed us to have several heart-to-heart conversations that I now value greatly. Among these, I remember discussions we had regarding suicide where she would, almost furiously, dispose her feelings on the idea. She barked at how selfish she found even the mere thought of one taking his or her own life. She dismissed the idea as an answer for anything and felt it was a direct slap in the face of anyone left to deal with the loss. It was very clear that she had no respect for anyone who chose that fate.

This conversation resumed any time news reports of a local or celebrity death to suicide emerged. Anyone who truly knew my mother knew her dislike for someone taking their own life. That's why one single future event left so many people in awe. It's also why I am still perplexed to this day.

I was raised in a Christian home. I won't go so far as to say that God was shoved down my and my brother's throats; however, we definitely knew not to step out of line. As a child, I loved attending church. But as a teen, I never understood the importance in building my own individual bond with God. My faith was susceptible to the weakness of those whom I idolized. I never looked to Him for my strength. Instead I looked to my parents or my pastors for that strength. Then I watched as a few individuals within the church turned the idea of God into something they used to judge others with and to enlighten their own existence. Church became a political battleground rather than a sanctuary, and my foundation crumbled without God as its stronghold.

By the time I hit twenty, I had become overly skeptical with the entire principle of church and religion. What I was reading from the Bible was far from what I witnessed within the church. Eventually, I became fed up with all the backstabbing I saw and gave up on attending any form of church. I still believed in God, just without the deluding human factor of it all.

Without God as my guide, I quickly turned to the world for inspiration and guidance. From there, my life slowly unraveled.

The next ten years came and went in a blurry haze; mostly due to the fact that I became an adamant partier. Though I did have some significant life-changing experiences such as joining the Air Force at twenty-one and getting married and having a child at twenty-six, alcohol established a permanent mainstay in my life. I wish I could say that I was a great husband and father in my early married years but that would be absolute fiction. Truth is, I was a mess. Extremely arrogant and self-indulgent, my wife and son took a back seat to my love for the bottle. I occasionally attempted to stop drinking and turn my life over to God, but with a severe preoccupation for concerning myself with only myself, God didn't stand much of a chance.

2

A Call I Never Imagined

April 17, 2006

I spent my early morning hours staring at a target down range through the sights of an M-16. It was my annual recertification, and so far things were going better than normal.

It was a beautiful day at Minot Air Force Base, North Dakota, and I was feeling pretty good. The weekend before was great, spending some needed relaxation time with my wife, Natalie, and our son, Steven. I also had the opportunity to call and speak with the rest of the family. My brother, Scotty, and his family were doing well in Dallas, and Dad and Mom had spent the weekend with friends at the river.

During the conversation with dad, I could hear mom in the background saying how excited she was about all the fish they had caught and how much she wished we could have been there. My father is a well-known catfisherman; He and my mother spent a great deal of time at the river cabin they had built from the ground up. Both of them sounded in good health and great spirits.

Knowing all is well with my family always helps me cope with life's issues. So for the most part, the morning had kick-started a fresh, lively new week.

After returning from lunch, I was prepping for the qualification round of shooting when I was called to the Instructor's pod. There, I was informed of an emergency at the fire station and I needed to report there as soon as possible.

Being a firefighter in the US Air Force, there are not many venues which take priority over my primary duties. However, annual M-16 qualification is one which does. So when I was informed of an emergency and instructed to return to the fire department immediately, I assumed there was a major fire and all firefighters were being recalled. But that thought quickly dissipated as I looked at the flashing messages on my phone in my truck. Scotty had called three times, all within the past forty minutes.

Now one thing to know about Scotty is that he is all business, especially while on the clock. For him to call in the middle of the day, and three times at that, meant this was no fire I was responding to.

Driving toward the fire station, I returned Scotty's call. His answer immediately told me something very bad had happened. "Where the hell are you?" Scotty demanded. I explained that I was on my way to the fire house for an emergency. He replied "But where are you?" I knew he was about to tell me of a serious issue with mom, dad, or both. I pleaded with him to let me get to the firehouse and hear it from them because I didn't know if I could keep the truck on the road if he was to tell me himself. He agreed that was best, and told me to call him the second I knew. Once he hung up, I quickly dialed Natalie at work and told her to meet me at the station immediately.

Walking into the fire department seemed to take forever. Each step seemed as if I was walking on a treadmill. I felt as if I was walking into a funeral home, but I didn't know who I was there to see.

As I entered the station, the Fire Chief's door opened and I saw a contingent of faces awaiting my arrival. The one face I didn't want to see was at the front of the pack ... my first sergeant. His being there told me my greatest fear had just become reality; one, or both, of my parents were dead. I made my way through the dreary crowd and sat down in the chair placed in the middle of the room. The first sergeant knelt down to my left and said "There's no easy way to say this so I'm just going to come right out and do it. Your mother is dead."

I could use the word "numb" to describe the feeling that came over me at that moment, but it wouldn't even come close. Actually, I can't even call it a feeling; I felt nothing. All I could say was "get me home." My deputy Chief asked, "Just you or all three?" Was that question even necessary? There was no way I could do this on my own. "All" I replied.

Just after, I felt Natalie's hand on my shoulder. She knelt down beside me with a look of fear, wanting to know, yet not wanting to know. As I said the words "Mom's dead," I remember feeling as if I was auditioning for a play, believing that the words spoken could in no way be true. The look on her face turned to stone. Natalie and mom were extremely close, and this heartbreak was felt by both of us.

As management scrambled to get the three of us to Texas, Natalie and I turned our focus on our son, Steven. How would we explain this to him? Granted, he was only two at the time, so it would be a few years before it would be necessary, but even so, it was a concern.

Natalie drove me to our friend's house where Steven was spending the day. I felt an uncontrollable amount of anxiety as I waited outside while she explained the situation to our friends.

In a matter of minutes, Natalie turned the corner with Steven in her arms. One look at him and I broke down. I fought to hold back the tears insisting that this was not the time. Clutching my son to my chest, surging waves of emotion crashed over me. All I could think of was having to someday explain the truth to him, whatever that might be. He would see the hundreds of pictures of them together and want to know where his "me-maw" was. What was I going to do?

We quickly loaded Steven in the car and headed toward the Airmen and Family Readiness Center to pick up our tickets. It was there that my anger absolutely went through the roof.

While Natalie made arrangements for the flight home, I started dialing anyone and everyone that might have some news. After countless calls, I finally reached mom's best friend, Bobby. The grief in her voice was undeniable when she answered the phone.

Bobby and mom had worked together for years and had become nearly inseparable. I knew this was absolutely killing her. She did her best to explain what they had been told so far. Investigators had been on the scene all day and had come to the conclusion that the wounds mom suffered were self-inflicted.

Sudden and inexplicable rage consumed me. There was no way anyone could make me believe my mother had taken her own life.

EXPLANATION: As I explained previously, Mom hated suicide. Anytime she heard of someone taking their own life, she became very angry and vocal about it. Knowing this, I refused to even entertain the idea of mom killing herself.

With rage in my voice, I asked what Dad's response, was but Bobby had not been there for that conversation. All she knew was the house was quickly roped off as a crime scene after investigators spoke with him.

Bobby did her best to calm me down, but there was no way that could happen. It was absolutely unfathomable that mom had killed herself. My body stayed tensed for hours after speaking with her.

Flight arrangements were made for early the next

morning so we returned home to pack.

Luckily Steven had fallen asleep earlier so he was unaware of what would happen once I entered the house. Once I passed through the front door, I tore through the house searching for any picture I could find of mom. Once I found one I lost every bit of emotion I had been holding back for hours. I fell to the floor, clutching the picture tightly to my chest. A searing pain raced through my left upper chest around my heart that would stay with me for months. Natalie wrapped her arms around me and held me for what seemed like hours.

Gradually I found the motivation to move again. "What can I do to help you? What do you need? What can help make this easier for you?" Natalie kept asking.

The only thing I could think of was Miller. Daniel Miller was a coworker and good friend. I knew having him and his wife, Denyse, there would help ease my agitation.

While Natalie called the Miller's on our cell phone, my house phone rang. I heard the worried voice of another coworker and good friend, Jessica Newbraugh. She told me the deputy chief had called to tell her what had happened. "I'm on my way; what do you need?" She asked. All I could think of was food because I knew neither Natalie nor I would have the time to fix dinner while we prepared for the trip. She agreed and quickly hung up.

With friends on the way, I was able to refocus. My phone calls back to Texas found everyone still puzzled, searching for answers. Dad was finally able to enter the house after some close friends cleaned up the area where mom was found. The detectives had not released their findings, but a meeting was scheduled for 4:00 PM the following day to discuss them.

The remainder of the night crawled at turtle speed. Friends arrived with food, breaking up the monotony of endless calls both to and from Texas. In my mind, I knew my mom had been murdered, though I fought hard not to go there. I had already ruled out the ridiculous suggestion of suicide.

Morning came and went in a blur of confusion, swallowed up in rainy, gray skies. I don't remember much of the flight home except for breaking down in tears at 28,000 feet with a cabin full of onlookers. Natalie did her best to restore my peace and calm, but it was nonexistent.

3

Landing in Dallas

We had decided to fly to Dallas to meet up with my brother, Scotty, and his family, stay the night at their house, and then trek down together to Bryan, Texas, to the home that now belonged solely to my father.

Stepping off that plane in Dallas seemed very odd; I didn't want to be making this trip; however, I was extremely happy to see Scotty. It was strange to see a smile on his face amongst all the pain he had to be feeling.

Natalie, Steven, and I quickly exchanged hugs with my brother and made our way to his car. I don't know if I've ever walked with more purpose than I did at that moment, for I knew that dad's meeting with the investigator had taken place over an hour before our landing. I had to know the conclusion of their findings.

My phone was connecting to dad's number before I even sat down in the car. There was an eerie mixture of relief and sadness in dad's voice when he answered the phone ... relief knowing we had made it to Dallas safely, and sadness from the news he would have to explain.

Dad expressed his relief that we were all together. He tried to hide the truth by simply saying, "go home and love one another tonight and I'll see you all in the morning."

My mind froze in a silent scream. I just spent the last twenty-four hours conjuring up everything imaginable about the mysterious death of my mother and now I am expected to wait another twenty-four hours to find out the truth? No way! I told dad I wasn't getting off the phone until he told me exactly what had happened. Dead silence fell over the phone as dad contemplated the words he would use. His response was simple, "Son, she left a note."

My heart sank to my feet. I could not believe the words that had just come out of his mouth. I whispered, "Please tell me it's not true."

Scotty, the genius that he is, took no time in figuring out what I had just been told. "She killed herself?" he asked for confirmation. I couldn't respond. I simply closed my eyes and held the phone tightly to my chest. My answer was obvious.

I spent the next thirty minutes sobbing through the phone, begging my father to tell me why. He had no answer. I asked if the investigators had even truly searched the scene. That's when he broke it all down for me.

When they returned home from their fishing trip Sunday night, Mom and Dad found that the air conditioner had broken while they were away. So Monday morning, dad called his air-conditioning technician, a friend of theirs who had been to the house on several occasions. He was to arrive at 9:30 AM to take a look at the unit. Dad went on to work, leaving mom at home to await the technician's arrival.

Sometime during that thirty minute interval, mom restocked the Dr. Pepper in the fridge for dad, washed dishes, changed clothes, wrote a note, and shot herself. Dad included more details in his story, but that was the essence of it. The story left me stupefied and speechless; yet unconvinced. The whole scenario left me with one overall question, "Mom, suicide; why?"

Dad did his best to ease my suffering, but there was no point; my foundation was shattered. No one was ever going to make me believe that my mother had taken her own life. It was simply unbelievable.

4

Don't Push Me

𝕣

The plan was to stay at Scotty and Megan's house for the night, then drive down to Bryan the next morning. I say "the plan;" at that point I had no plan. I didn't know what I had at that point. I had just gone from being a thirty-year-old man, who had the world on an oyster, to being decimated; to being made a survivor to the one thing I never expected by the one person I could have never imagined.

That whole afternoon at Scotty's passed in an overwhelming blur. Everyone tried to be happy to see each other again, yet no one knew how to express the underlying devastation of emotions boiling beneath the surface. It was as surreal as surreal could get.

The one thing we did do, which we all knew was unwise, was crack open a case of beer while we allowed our emotions to surface. This proved to be an incredibly bad decision.

Growing up, Scotty was always the tougher, sportier, and cooler-under-pressure type of guy. I played the perfect younger brother role of "momma's boy," the more emotionally challenged of the two, who never missed a moment to hide under mom's wing when trouble arose. Knowing this, Scotty had already planned to test my emotions while at his house because he wanted to ensure that I was ready for anything overly distressing that would be placed in front of us upon arrival in Bryan. While I now understand his intentions; at that time all he did was expose my innermost demons.

After dinner that night and at least halfway into the case of beer, Scotty initiated his plan by expressing his expectations of what was soon to come. He left no stone unturned as he rifled through all the thoughts rushing through his mind. He was ready for anything and everything to hit the fan. I could tell through his demeanor and body language that he was going to take it all head on.

But the mood changed suddenly when he started putting pressure on me. He wanted to see where my head was because he felt that if I wasn't emotionally prepared, the next few days might take me along with mom. The intensity of his questions grew as the frustration started to fall on me like rain. The turmoil of the last twenty-four hours and the affects of the beer both started to crush in on me. I remember feeling an overwhelming amount of anger toward his continued badgering. Finally, in the kitchen of their house, it all came to a head. Looking back, I can't remember which straw finally broke the camel's back, but once it hit, there was no stopping it.

I lunged at Scotty with both fists hitting him square in the middle of his chest, landing him hard on the tile floor. Megan started yelling at me as I stood over him with clinched fists. It only took seconds for Scotty to bounce back off the floor and deliver a decent counter shove. The noise escalated from subtle to ferocious, waking Natalie from the other side of the house. Scotty and I fought our way outside to continue the stupidity of what had become an all-out brawl. It was like two lions waging war. I wanted to rip him apart for causing the rage in me. He wanted to do the same for hitting him unexpectedly.

I have tried to remember the entire scenario that played out in the front yard of their home, but the rage had blinded me; all I recall is seeing red. I know many blows were taken and dealt, though none violent enough to settle the score. Eventually, our wives pulled us back in the house and into separate rooms to put some distance between us.

I clung to Natalie, using her shoulder as a crying towel, pouring out every tear within me. All my rage and emotions surfaced. It wasn't necessarily rage toward Scotty; it was rage for being in the moment all together. I wept harder than I had ever wept before, repeating, "Why, why?" The confusion, frustration, and desperation of the last twenty-four hours had finally broken me to a point that I could barely function. The tears continued to fall until I passed out from sheer exhaustion.

Waking up the next morning with a dismal outlook for what was to come of that day, I figured Natalie, Steven, and I would be finding a different means of transportation to Bryan being that I had blatantly attacked my brother the night before. But much to my surprise, I was met with a gentle "good morning" from Scotty as I entered the kitchen. There was no remorse, or ill-tempered feelings on his part. He had done what he thought was best the night before. He surfaced my embroiled emotions before we reached Bryan because he knew the outcome would be far worse if I went in to that environment with a loaded gun, so to speak.

We barely spoke about the night before. It was simple "I'm sorrys" from both sides. Neither one of us had any intentions of continuing the battle because we knew the real fight was still to come. We were brothers, and we had handled the situation like brothers. Nothing else was necessary.

I often look back on that night and try to imagine what might have happened if Scotty hadn't purged my anger as he did. I truly believe that his attack on my emotions saved me a lot more heartache throughout the following weeks.

NOTE: This situation may seem barbaric to you, the reader, but Scotty showed his love and concern for me by allowing me to beat it out of him. He showed me the true importance of being brothers.

5

Arriving in Bryan

The drive to Bryan was the most somber three-hour period of my life. There were no smiles, no singing to the music on the radio, nothing. Even with three kids in the car, the trip was mundane as hell.

At first I thought the silence and uncomfortable feeling in the car was due to the fight from the night before. But I quickly realized that we were all preparing ourselves for what was to come. The fight was done; there was nothing else to be said of it. Now, we were just minutes away from what could quite possibly be one of the hardest moments we would ever experience ... when we would walk into the house where mom killed herself.

I have searched for the words to describe that feeling of driving up to the house: emptiness, cold, numb; those come close but still are so far away.

Dad had basically been standing at the door awaiting our arrival since dawn. In a heartbeat, he was standing at the car as we filed out one by one. He gave quaint greetings toward the others, but grabbed Scotty and me as soon as he had the chance. The embrace lasted minutes, with no words exchanged; none were necessary.

Walking into the house was odd. Mom was always a meticulous housekeeper, and by the look of things you couldn't even tell she was gone. Everything was in its exact place, just as it had been for years.

Making my way through the house, I saw many faces, some familiar and some not, all giving their condolences. At that point I was only thinking of one thing; getting to the chair. In dad's recollections of the last time he saw her alive, mom was sitting in the recliner in the workout room before he left for work. I needed to see it … to be there where she had been.

I turned the corner from the kitchen into the den and there it was, same as always. I sat down in it, feeling like a child again. I was hoping and praying to feel mom's arms around me, holding me tightly. I felt nothing; nothing but an eerie emptiness that would consume the house for months to come.

I sat there in silence for a few minutes until dad walked in the room, worry and pain etched across his face. He knelt in front of me, placing his forearms on my knees. It only took him looking me in the eyes for a few seconds for me to break down, hard. He didn't say a word, he just let me cry.

Sometime later after most of the visitors had left us alone, dad sat me, Scotty, Megan, and Natalie down for a talk. I had an idea of what was coming, but there was no way to prepare for what happened next. Dad pulled a letter from a protective sleeve and unfolded it. He began reading it aloud.

> Dad,
> you have been a wonderful husband & to me & loving Father to our sons. I am so sorry for all the pain I have caused to everyone who loves me.
> I can't stand the lies & deceit & madness going on in my head anymore.

(Copy of my mother's suicide note)

A stunned expression draped across each of our faces. What lies? What deceit? What madness? We all heard the words but none of us could fathom what they meant. We sat there for a while, trying to decipher the puzzle that had just been laid out in front of us. There were no concrete answers then, nor is there now, years later. Sure, we can hypothesize, but she took her truth with her to the grave, forever leaving a piece of the puzzle lost.

6

The Funeral Home

The next two days were spent at the Hillier Funeral Home in Bryan. There, all the obligatory decisions were made as to the casket, the viewing, the obituary, and everything else that loved ones are called upon to make.

It was pretty obvious the funeral home staff was aware of the way mom died because of the way they tip-toed around certain questions and topics. I am not a fan of funerals or funeral homes, but I was extremely impressed by their professionalism and facilities. They truly seemed to care about the way Mom was represented.

There were lots of discussions and decisions made on the first day. I vividly remember when it was time to choose the casket. Dad left it up to me and Scotty to decide what we wanted. Though I never dreamed I would have to make such a decision, in all honesty it was one of the easiest I ever did. Mom loved roses … we all knew that. Scotty and I walked around; he took the right side of the roomwhile I took the left. Turning the corner, we found it at the same time … a burgundy casket with engraved, painted roses on all four corners. Scotty signaled Dad. There was a glimmer of a smile on his face as soon as Dad saw it. Laying his hands on the outside of the wooden box, the decision was made. What I thought would be the hardest part of the whole situation, ended up being the easiest.

The rest of the day came and went rather quickly. There

were enough decisions and conversations to keep us all busy. Dad made it fairly obvious to the funeral home staff that this was a combined effort. It wasn't just dad making the decisions, but Scotty and me as well. I don't know if dad was just having a hard time making all the decisions or if he truly wanted our help. Either way, it humbled and honored me knowing I had some say in the way my mother's body would be laid to rest. That is one thing I'll always appreciate.

The last thing that had to be decided that day was whether or not there would be an open-casket viewing. This was by far the hardest part of this entire process.

Joining hands, the family crossed the space with much trepidation. Anxiety weighed heavily on my chest. The approach to the casket seemed to lengthen with every step. A short walk which only took seconds seemed to take hours and the closer we got, the more anxiety bore down on my chest.

Once we finally reached the casket I looked down on a woman dressed in my mother's clothes. I say a woman because the figure in that coffin looked absolutely nothing like my mother. My mother was beautiful, with a constant smile on her face. The woman in that coffin had a permanent frown, a facial expression none of us recognized. The damage from the bullet had caused her face to swell, further distorting her features.

I wish I had not looked in that coffin. That was not the last image of my mother that I wanted ingrained in my head. I certainly didn't want it to be the last image for others who knew her. It was a unanimous "no" from all family members; the casket would stay closed. No one needed to remember her that way.

7

The Wake

From the time we landed in Dallas, I had been suffering from an intense pain encompassing the entire left side of my chest. I simply chalked this up to the extreme amount of stress endured over the past few days. But as we arrived at the funeral home the night of Mom's viewing, the pain went from intense to excruciating. Massaging it helped a little, but at this point I was almost clawing my chest. I knew I had to stay there, but I was worried at how much more of this pain I could endure.

We met with the staff to ensure everything was in order. And everything was, until they opened the doors to the viewing room. One of the staff members who had completed final details on Mom's body before she was ultimately laid to rest had forgotten to close the lid to the casket. Up to that point I had wondered if I was the only person disturbed by seeing her earlier in the day; I quickly learned I was not alone. Everyone loudly let the staff know that the casket lid was to be closed immediately. To say it was an outburst is a huge understatement. No one wanted to view whoever that was laying in Mom's casket again.

Once everything was in order, we all stood talking quietly until we were told a few vehicles had pulled up outside, what was some thirty minutes early. We walked out the door to see Mom's brothers and their families filing out of three large vehicles. They had driven from as far as Illinois, and I could see the discomfort etched in their faces as they exited their vehicles. Everyone tried to muster smiling faces as we welcomed them, but fake smirks were all that resulted.

With quiet murmurs of sympathy, we made our way inside the funeral home. To use the word "uncomfortable" with what happened next is an enormous understatement. The brothers were quite upset that they would not be allowed to see their sister's body and say their goodbyes. At one point I thought it was going to be a battle royal because the brothers weren't accepting no for an answer. But we held to our decision to keep the casket closed. Eventually they calmed down, but it was clear they were not happy with the decision.

After tempers simmered, we all did our best to maintain what composure we had left to greet the hundreds of people who filed in to the funeral home. Face after face, person after person, condolence after condolence—is it really supposed to make things better? If it is, it did not work.

I tried my best to stay at the door, greeting people as they arrived. I wanted nothing to do with the viewing room. Attached at the hip was my long-time friend, Brandon Ballard. Brandon and I became friends early during high school and had remained tight even while I was serving abroad. Brandon had known my mother quite well and was devastated when he heard the news. I could tell he had no idea what to say. Instead, he let his sympathies and loyalty be known by shadowing me for the next few days.

About an hour into the viewing, one of the staff asked me to come in the office. Followed by Brandon, I made my way to a room where two other staff members were waiting. One of the ladies explained that they were extremely worried about me and questioning if they should call the paramedics to have me checked out. I hadn't noticed, but the clawing of my chest had become a constant action, so much so that the entire staff had noticed. I explained the pain had started three days before and that even though it hurt I would be fine. I thanked the ladies for their concern and assured them I would be alright. I spent the rest of the night masking my pain and trying my best not to let it show.

Finally, all the visitors had come and gone and we were relieved to have an end to the long and exhausting day's events. However, our relief would be extremely short lived as we had to prepare for the next day: Mom's funeral service and burial.

8

The Funeral

After numerous attempts and failures to recreate the events from mom's funeral, I have decided that some things are truly better left unsaid. The only comment I will give is this:

Al Jolly, minister and long time friend of the family, did a magnificent job of remembering Mom as she was ... an incredible mother, a loving and supportive wife, a servant to many, and a hater of none. He perfectly painted the portrait of Mom's inner and outer beauty and her steadfast love for the next generation of Thomases—her grandchildren. In short, it was a perfect reflection of Mom; sweet, simple and gracious.

9

Back to Minot

🍂

We spent a total of two weeks in Bryan; most of which were used to assist dad in figuring out how to manage things around the house which mom had maintained. Staying there wasn't easy, but it proved to be better than what would happen once we returned to North Dakota.

The flight back to Minot was more miserable than words can describe. I was still numb and definitely not ready to be away from the family so soon after.

Prior to landing, the pilot came over the intercom to inform us of the weather conditions—cold, wet, gray skies; all weather conditions that a person dealing with a mountains worth of depression didn't need.

As the airplane started to descend, I took a mental picture of the sun, knowing it would be at least a month before I saw it again. The descent through the clouds was a color chart from bright blue to dark gray. Sure, I had seen the gray skies of Minot before, but this was different. This was a saturating gray. This was a gray that looked like it could choke the life out of the sun if given the chance. It was absolutely paralyzing, and any chance of an optimistic outlook on life was choked away as well.

I remember very little about landing and the ride back to base. What I do remember is standing at the kitchen sink staring out the back window soon after we returned home. I stood there wondering how I was supposed to start life over again. I remember talking to Mom in my head and telling her to leave space for me because I'd be with her soon.

Natalie, as always, was worried. She asked what I needed, what I wanted. She was ready to do anything just to assist me in my healing process. "Friends" I said, "as many as may want to come over, get them here."

Almost immediately people started pouring in the door. We had at least fifteen to twenty folks over within ten minutes, mostly firefighters.

Now one thing to understand about firefighters is that when a brother is hurting, they do whatever they have to do to make it right. One buddy asked what I wanted, and I told him that I wanted to drink a beer with my friends in my mother's memory. When you have brothers like this, be careful what you ask for. Before I knew it, there was beer stacked all around my kitchen. There was so much beer that the refrigerator was filled to capacity and we still had more to go around. Needless to say, the next few days are hard to remember.

Night three after returning to Minot started the same as the two before ... plenty of friends and plenty of beer. This was one of those situations where Natalie was basically allowing me to do whatever I wanted. She never even asked me to slow down on drinking; she simply let me be.

Now everyone knows that medicating depression with a depressant—alcohol in this case—only leads to bad things. I was getting there fast.

In those three days, beer was much like money, gone before I knew it. In no time at all, I found myself easily around the twenty-fifth beer mark ... only I felt nothing. Trekking to the fridge for yet another beer, I found a near empty case with only one remaining. I held it up in celebratory fashion and hollered, "Killed another one, boys." With an array of claps and cheers from my friends, I threw the empty case in the corner with the others.

Steven, who had probably seen more those last three days than he needed to, was taking it all in. He quickly picked up the discarded case and brought it back to me. Following the unintended directions he had received all night he asked me, "Daddy, do you want a beer?" Playfully, I replied, "Yes, I would." Reaching into the box, he pulled out a "pretend" beer. "Here ya' go Daddy," he said.

Taking the imaginary can, I said, "Thank you, son" and pretended to drink it. He said, "Okay, one for you and one for me." And using the exact same gestures he learned from me, he too drank his imaginary beer. It was like somebody slapped me with sobriety; I was as alert as I had been in weeks. I realized that my actions were all being recorded in the mind of my two-year-old son. The proverbial light bulb went on over my head.

With this newfound revelation still fresh in my mind, I announced to all within range that this was not the right thing for me to do. I had a friend take all the remaining alcohol from the house. Natalie, puzzled by my actions, asked what was up. I told her if I continued this way I would soon be gone as well. I had to find a different way other than alcohol to deal with this moment in my life.

As all the friends and beer quickly and quietly left the premises, Steven and I laid together on the couch in front of the television. I told Natalie we were going to chill, relax without alcohol, and start the next day with a fresh outlook. Little did I know at the time, but this bout with alcohol was just beginning.

NOTE: To friends of survivors: I know you want to comfort your bereaving pal in any way possible; however, try to come up with different avenues than bringing over case after case of beer. At the time, it was a welcome relief from the nightmarish two weeks; however, it almost proved to be my demise.

10

The Morning After

Ohe next morning, I awakened to the realization that I needed help.

Natalie woke me up with a fresh, large cup of coffee. We sat back and discussed the next chapter of life we were about to open. During this time I downed the first sixteen ounces of coffee and started on my second.

NOTE: One important thing to know about alcohol and alcohol withdraws is that caffeine greatly increases its symptoms, especially on an empty stomach. Knowing that fact, you can see where three days of straight alcohol consumption followed by thirty-two ounces of coffee, an empty stomach, and an insurmountable amount of depression could possibly cause erratic behavior. It did just that, and then some.

At the end of my second cup, Natalie left for work. Immediately after, Steven woke up and joined me in the kitchen where I was cleaning up from all the festivities. I gave him a Pop-tart and set him on the counter where he liked to watch me when I cooked.

Before I realized what was happening, an extreme cloud of depression surrounded me and I felt as if I was suffocating in fear. I became weak in the knees and collapsed on the floor in front of the sink. My heart felt as if it would burst out of my chest and I enfolded my legs, shaking from hard chills. This was the first time in my life that I actually heard voices in my head. The voices were repeating words spoken at Mom's funeral.

My heart was racing a mile a minute. Soon thereafter I started to see images ... death in its unspoken form. One of the primary images was of me hanging from a rescue rope attached to the top of the crash stalls in the Minot Fire Department. My eyes were wide open staring straight back at me while my mouth was moving saying the words "come with me," only in my Mother's voice. (That image haunted me for the next year as I worked in that station.)

Steven, still sitting on the kitchen counter, started calling my name. I remember looking up at him and visualizing his face covered with blood. His voice was his own stating, "It's okay daddy; it's okay."

I remember fear, unbridled, relentless, overwhelming fear. The rush of emotions had brought on an extreme panic attack. I knew that I had to get help immediately for both me and my son.

I picked up the phone and dialed the first number I thought of. Within two rings, Amy Dalton, the wife of one of my fellow firefighters, answered. She could tell something was wrong, and told me to hold tight and keep talking to her; Brandon was on his way.

The nice thing about living on a military installation is that there's always someone close by. Within minutes, I heard Brandon's truck door shut and watched as he came in the front door. The first thing he did was get Steven down from the cabinet, who, by this time, had started to panic. Then Brandon knelt down beside me and said, "I'm here man. I've got you; you're not going anywhere." I told him of the visions I had been having and that I knew exactly what was wrong. I told him I needed food and I needed a few beers to counteract the alcohol withdrawals. His reply was solid and comforting; "No problem, brother; Brandon's here for you."

He quickly bundled Steven and I up and ushered us outside to his awaiting truck. I know he made a few phone calls, but I was too dazed at the time to pay attention. Next thing I knew, we were pulling into the bowling alley on Minot AFB. Later I would realize the genius behind his choice of hangouts; good food, cold beer, and throwing the ball down the lane definitely helped improve my symptoms.

Later joined by his wife and another friend, he kept me there for hours making sure that my head had cleared and my symptoms had all but ceased.

NOTE: There are few times in this book that you'll hear me speak of people who would save my life; Brandon was the first. He refused to leave my side until he knew Natalie had me and I had emotionally come back down to earth. Thanks Brandon.

11

Seeking Help

Five days after arriving back in Minot, I knew it was time to seek professional help. Things were happening to me that I could not control. I knew I had to take that step and ask for help.

I decided to call One Source, an assistance tool Air Force members can use for all types of unexpected situations. Once the craziness from the day prior had subsided I made the call and was set up with an appointment to a doctor downtown that would hopefully help me sort out all the junk in my head.

Inside the doctor's office, I laid out the entire situation with Mom's suicide, the unresolved questions buzzing around my head, the intolerable chest pains, and the fact that I had spent the past three nights pointlessly attempting to drown it all.

It didn't take him long to start rattling off the normal propaganda you might get from any doctor facing a patient with the same issues. But he surprised me when he suggested I check into the hospital. Of all the things I expected to hear, that was a suggestion I didn't see coming.

He explained that the magnitude of loss I had experienced had left deep scars that were still fresh. He was concerned not only with my emotional response but also my physical reactions, present and future. He assured me this would be a step in the right direction. He reminded me that Mom was already gone and that I could do nothing to bring her back. My focus at that moment had to be about me; it had to be about fixing what had been broken by her loss before it took an irreparable toll.

At first I was totally put off with his idea. I was afraid of being treated as a mental patient. I had no idea what type of patient I was, I just knew I was hurting and I could not make the pain go away. The more I considered the suggestion, the more I began to realize that it was the only choice I had at the time.

As with all major decisions affecting the family, I wanted to consult Natalie first. I excused myself to make the call. Natalie, still searching and praying for any means to comfort me, agreed that doing this would probably be the best choice. Reluctantly, I accepted. I had no clue that decision would initially make things much worse, yet eventually be my saving grace.

That afternoon runs through my brain like a mouse on a wheel ... spinning out of control with no true direction, no plotted course, and no clue of a destination. I was stuck, poked, and prodded with every instrument the medics could find. I was EKGd, evaluated, and x-rayed like a frog on a dissecting board. The doctors and nurses eagerly searched for a symptom no microscope could find. I was ailing from and living with a broken heart, plain and simple.

Everything was calm at first. Doctors and nurses alike seemed concerned, not at all edgy or standoffish; that came later. Initially, I was given a normal room with a bed, TV, and windows. But as I was just getting comfortable, two orderlies came in and said I was being moved to intensive care because of the reasons for admittance, one of those being a suicide attempt.

What? I was livid! At what time did I ever say I was even considering suicide, much less attempting it? That answer would be "never." Somewhere along the way I had gone from being an individual who wanted help dealing with the emotions after my mother's suicide, to being the person trying to commit suicide. Understandably, the rest of this picture does not paint well for my mental well-being.

Once in intensive care, thankfully accompanied by my wife, I was placed in the bed directly across from the nurses' station with privacy curtains opened as wide as possible. The first nurse brought in a sedative to calm me down and make me feel more relaxed. Problem here! I was completely relaxed up until I was branded a suicide threat! Regardless, the sedative was administered, making only a few events of the evening stand out in my memory.

First, I was informed I was being transferred to the 3C wing, formally known as the Mental Ward, on suicide watch. My mind raced, trying to remember what could have made the counselor think I had suicidal thoughts. Nothing came to mind. The suicide discussion related to my mother's death, not one I was contemplating!

Second, I learned that due to my alcohol binge, I would be forced to spend the next month in an inpatient substance abuse program. Now I knew the real reason for the sedative ... to keep me calm as I learned what their intentions were for me. Drugs or no drugs, I knew separating me from my wife and child for a month was not going to be beneficial. But it was out of my hands now. While checking into the hospital was my decision, following doctor's orders was not. In the military, you either agree or face military punishment. Needless to say, I quickly changed my opinion on how helpful checking into the hospital was going to be.

Natalie spent the next hour or so trying to comfort me. I can't remember if it worked; actually, I can't remember anything after that point.

12

3C

To say the least, I was dazed and confused when they moved me from intensive care to the mental ward. I was a zombie: semi-comatose and numb. I felt nothing for I had nothing left to feel. My mother was dead by her own hand, and I was on my way to what I thought was a thirty-day sentence away from my wife and son. I was lost, desperate, and alone.

My stay at 3C is sketchy, probably due to the continual dosing of sedatives. I do, however, remember the staff to be extremely nice and caring. I don't know what access they had to my file but I do remember one of them telling me I had no reason for being there. She was somewhat apologetic for all that had happened and assured me that if I simply "played the game" I would be back with my family in no time.

I didn't know specifics of the other patients there, but I do know it was the most uncomfortable I have ever been. I had nothing in common with any of them, or at least I hoped. I couldn't believe that in a matter of three weeks, I had gone from on top of the world to being a patient in a mental facility. It was the stuff of which movies are made.

While there, Natalie brought Steven up to see me. It was good to see them, but I knew it would be short lived.

The days came and went at turtle speed. In one of my writings immediately following my release I wrote, *"Time stands still in a mindless prison where fear and desperation are a welcomed distraction."* I only spent a total of three full days there, but it felt like an eternity.

My release was bitter sweet. Even though I was being released from one asylum, my confinement was not over ... there was still rehab.

Very few people ever knew about my time spent in 3C; it's not something for which I want to be remembered. In hindsight, I can see the rationale of the medical staff looking at me from the outside. I was crushed, decimated, and not even I knew what I was capable of if left alone during that time of utter confusion.

13

CDU

I remember the drive to rehab that first morning like it was yesterday. I was nervous as a teenager on a first date. My hands were so sweaty I had to wipe them off just to maintain control of the vehicle. I had no clue what to expect. There were two things, however, that brought a small smile to my face. First, the thirty-day inpatient treatment actually was only fifteen days plus weekends. Second, the doctor in the base mental health clinic decided it would be better for the entire family if I remained an outpatient, meaning I was able to attend treatment during the day and spend the nights at home.

Walking into the chemical dependency unit (CDU) felt like walking into a new school for the first time in the middle of the year. I was extremely skeptical about being forced to go to chemical dependency treatment; after all, to my knowledge it wasn't the alcohol that had led me there in the first place. I felt very alone and out of place. The rooms looked gloomy and depressing ... not at all happy or appealing. Each person I passed in the hallway seemed to mirror my feelings.

My perception changed, however, when I was greeted by an extremely warm and welcoming staff: three ladies I would come to consider as friends by the end of my treatment. They asked how I was, explained all the rules and told me of the daily schedule. They did a very good job of putting me at least somewhat at ease.

Then they did something I did not expect; something that would ultimately change my life and be the starting point to what you are reading today. They gave me a simple seventy-five-page spiral notebook and a pen. Writing my feelings would help me release some of life's frustrations, they explained. I don't know why I hadn't thought of this. I love to write and have scribbled ideas down for years. I began looking at my situation in a whole new light and felt excitement for the first time since Mom's death. They unknowingly reminded me of one of my true loves ... one that would eventually bring me out of the depths of despair to which I had sunk.

NOTE: Due to confidentiality issues and respect for those I attended treatment with; I will refrain from expanding on discussion sessions. The rest of this section will center primarily on excerpts from my treatment notebook written during and soon after my release from CDU.

WARNING: Please realize that I was dealing with a ton of personal issues at this point in my life. I have changed some of the language initially used, yet the overall feelings are still evident.

CDU: Day 1

What am I doing here? How did life get so screwed up in such little time? Why is this happening to me; happening to my family? Why ... why, Mom?

The night after Day 1 CDU:

I made it through my first day of treatment. I was right; nobody gives a damn about what happened to Mom. All they care about is the alcohol. How am I supposed to concentrate on anything other than my mother, her death, and the way her death came to be? I can't. I won't.

CDU: Day 2

Basic day so far. Extremely gloomy outside; definitely doesn't help with my depression. Very few thoughts of Mom this morning. I'm afraid too much attention will be given to the drinking, which is a problem, but not the most important problem. Mom's suicide sucks. I need someone to concentrate on her death rather than my addictions. I can deal with the addiction; her death is killing me.

Setting sun

Long-awaited setting sun, steal all light till light is none. Show the darkness of the night to hide all fears from dawn's daylight. Close our eyes so we may sleep in peace and harmony where you keep. Protect us from the boogieman; guide us to the man of sand. Chase all nightmares far away; Rest us easy where we lay. Give us dreams so pure and sweet make them real some day to meet. Don't go so fast nor stay too long, for tomorrow brings a different song of work to do and people to see. Then again you'll come with another dream.

It's still gloomy outside. How do you fight depression when you live in the state it was born in?

EXPLANATION: As I will explain in another chapter, Minot, North Dakota, is a nice town and one in which I now have very fond memories of. But for someone raised in Texas where it is normally sunny, Minot can be a little depressing, especially when facing the issues such as mine. From around mid-September to mid-April the temperature in Minot is either near or below freezing and the sky remains a dreary shade of grey. Not easy living conditions for a person already drenched in depression, I assure you.

Ink from the pen bleeds onto the page, leaving puddles of confusion and misunderstanding. The fingers of the hand grip the pen in furry, enraged that the words refuse to reveal themselves. The mind tries to express its outrage of its current situation with no encouraging conclusion. Concentration is continually disrupted by grief's stupidity. The body fights endlessly, frightened of rebelling to a lonely place of dying. But why shouldn't the body or mind reject submittal for the one which all trust was handed to chose death's path? The whole did all to be a reflection of trust's keeper, so why shouldn't the whole wither into the passing dust? The question has pondered in my mind for years, yet she was the victim to its call. Damn you, conscience! Where were you in her final minutes? Why do you haunt me while you allowed her to slip so idly by? Am I more important in this life than she? Never! Then why did you sleep as she decided for us all what we must suffer and hurt and blame ourselves for? Where were you when you were needed most?

One of the first tenets we were taught in treatment was to find a "higher power." This was not a faith-based treatment facility, so the pushing of "God" in one essential form was not allowed. Even though I believed in God as my higher power, others did not. Regardless, their point remains that your "higher power" is important in helping you attain peace and allow you to recognize personal limitations.

Their pushing of a "higher power" also helped me to establish a bond with God. Though it took years to matriculate, my now-solidified relationship with Him initially sprouted roots during my time at CDU.

CDU: Day 3
A new day: and what a beautiful day it is! It's amazing the difference a new morning with sunshine can have on your spirits. I'm refreshed and ready to do and accomplish what you lead me to do, God. Bring it on!

An unpredicted outcome; I'm beginning to find sanity within the walls of a drunken prison. The devil I have become may just lead me to the friends which will save my life.

EXPLANATION: I thought I would be alone while in treatment, having no one with whom I could relate. Quite the contrary; I met a number of new friends during my time there. One thing my counselor said always stuck with me; "Drunks are the nicest people you'll ever meet." In all honesty, he was right. I got along with most other patients there, and they helped me to finally realize just how much of a drinking problem I truly had.

My God above watches over me as I turn away.
He holds his hand out to me, begging me to stay.
He offers any blessing that he could ever give.
He shows me the door to eternal life, hoping that I might live.
But like an idiot, I keep walking backwards, turning from the light choosing a life full of hurt and pain over a life of living right.
I know my life is messed up still I choose to go astray, thinking I'll still have the chance to live right if I wait another day.

What I say is me is really not me at all.
I search to find out who I am but I find nothing.
But what am I looking for anyway?
Am I looking for the person I truly am or someone I want to be?
Am I looking for a goal in my life or an obstacle I have?
And what if I do find myself?
Will I like myself?
And if I don't, what do I do then?
God, this is confusing.
All I know is that I don't want to be me anymore.

What is hell? To me, hell is wandering life pointlessly; having no idea what my purpose is. Waking up at thirty realizing you're lost in your position in life—Yes, I have a wife and a son and a good job, but what am I supposed to do in life that will leave an impression on the world?

EXPLANATION: I have always believed every person is put on this earth for a purpose. Some people respond to their designed purpose while others do not. Before Mom's death, I had never found or understood my purpose. While I lived a good life, I always thought I was destined to do more. But after her death, I started to visualize just what my purpose was. That journey will be discussed later in this book.

Within my writings from treatment, I started composing personal notes to Mom; simple conversations between a mother and son. These random writings still continue from time to time. Some are gentle and warm; others, not so much.

Morning Mom,

I woke up less angry than I was when I turned in. God, I wish I could give you a huge hug and kiss. I miss that. My heart hurts, troubled from missing you so. Please don't hate me when I get angry that you left. I can't control my feelings right now. I just can't. No matter how my mood swings may change my feelings, please know that I love you so much. I miss you more than I miss my sanity.

Love,
Nelson

<u>*CDU: Day 4*</u>
Thank God for another beautiful day. Spoke with Dad for half an hour this morning. He seems to be doing well, but I can occasionally hear despair in his voice. He's been having me read Job. I see his point; Job went through a hell of a lot more than I have and never turned from God so why should I? Religion is becoming easier to handle with each passing day. I don't blame God for taking Mom, but I am jealous that he has her and we don't.

EXPLANATION: I've heard other's ideas on what happens to people who kill themselves. Quite frankly, I don't care. I choose not to judge, especially when it comes to Heaven and Hell. I feel that I have plenty to concern myself with in my personal struggles with temptation; who am I to pick up a stone? Mom was a God-fearing woman and tried, emphatically, to follow in his path. Other's personal interpretation of what the Bible says about suicide is their own opinion. For me, I know that I would not be where I am today if Mom hadn't of gone the way she did. God's purpose for me was eventually revealed through that situation, which tells me that he had a purpose for her loss that way as well.

Mother's Day 2006:

Dear Mom,

Happy Mother's Day; No offense but you don't deserve it right now. Who was I supposed to call today? Did you ever think of that? Dad, Scotty, and I will never look at Mother's Day the same, ever. Thanks for that. Thanks for leaving us. We'll never be the same again.

Bye

CDU: Day 5
It is another gloomy day here in Minot, North Dakota. God, I hate this state. The sun seems to show just enough to make you smile, then disappears again.

I'm in a little bit of a bad mood this morning. Yesterday was Mother's Day, and Wednesday will be Mom's one-month anniversary since she killed herself. Using terms of suicide in conjunction with my mother just doesn't seem real. What a selfish, despicable act from such a wonderful woman. Life just doesn't seem real anymore.

Depression is a cancer, slowly eroding the fundamental sanctity of the human spirit. It is a monster fixated on normalcy's consumption with the ultimate goal of killing one's willingness to live.

CDU: Day 7
Morning Mom,

I miss you, I miss you, I miss you; Just to let you know.

I picked up some beautiful pictures of your grandson yesterday; oh what a blessing he is. He talks about you all of the time. He misses his Me-Maw. You used to be so proud of him. You loved taking him out on the boat and taking pictures of him. God, you loved him. Why did you leave him? Why did you leave me with the horrible task of having to tell my son that his grandmother who loved him so much did something so tragic? I'm not mad at you right now; I just need you to send me the words to explain to him what happened. Actually, while you're at, it could you help me understand as well?

Love,
Nelson

Spoke with Dad today. He said he had a revelation. He said he realized that Mom didn't give him a choice in what's happened. He has no choice but to go on with his life, and he's preparing himself to do that. Good for you, Dad.

Mom,

Today's your one-month anniversary; congratulations. I hope you're proud. In one month you've reduced everything I've built my life on to meaningless rubble. I hope Dad moves on with his life; maybe he'll find someone who'll stick around this time. Scott and Meg are about to buy a new house. We'll probably throw a lot of birthday parties there. Just to let you know, you're not invited. You left. No, you didn't divorce Dad and move to another town; you died. You left by killing yourself. You gave us all fifty-three years of beauty just to turn it into a life time of hell. I love you, but goodbye. I'm spent.

Nelson

Thank God for me being an outpatient because these white walls are starting to bug the crap out of me. It feels so good to be able to come and go as I please. The sun is so much more beautiful by not having to see it through a hospital window all the time.

CDU: Day 8

It's half beautiful, half gloomy today; my negative attitude doesn't make it any better. I had a hard time waking up this morning. I just don't want to be here today. Either I'm still upset about yesterday being Mom's one-month anniversary, or I want to prepare food for Natty's birthday. Nat's twenty-four today. She's probably aged twenty years in the past month; she's been through so much yet been so supportive at the same time. She's been upset lately that she only had four years with Mom. She loved Mom. It scares me sometimes just how much the two are alike. They shop alike, dress alike, and care alike. God, it's got to be hard on her. My mood swings lately haven't helped I'm sure. The doctor has put me on Wellbutrin and it has disrupted my normalcy. I try to handle the pressure, but it's been hard. It's supposed to be hard ... I've lost my words.

CDU: Day 9

It's a beautiful day today. Again, that helps with my mood swings—plus, it's Friday, and I have the entire weekend to spend with Natalie and Steven. Excitement overwhelms me at this point. Being with them reminds me that there is still goodness in the world.

0910

It bothers me sitting here having to listen to patients and parents go back and forth about their problems and know that I've only got one parent left. Lately, I've had a hard problem dealing with the whys and what fors of Mom's suicide. I wish she would have picked up the phone and called someone for help. I wish she would have thought about just how much she was going to hurt us before she did something so drastic.

Mom, I wish you were here to bust my chops about my drinking. I know how much you hated me drinking—Scotty too. I guess I used alcohol to cover up my problems. You used exercise to cover yours; but it didn't help did it? I let my feelings out. Yes, I yell and bitch sometimes, but at least I get it out.

EXPLANATION: The further I went in CDU the more I started to realize that alcohol was probably more of a problem than I had made it out to be.

Sunday, May 21
A little frustrated today; I want to be in Texas with Pop, Scotty, and the family. I love spending time with Nat and Steven; I just wish the three of us could pack up and go. I hate this place; I'll never call Minot home. Natalie and I are arguing slightly because she wants me to stay in the military, and I just want to go back to Texas. I've loved my career, but I couldn't care less about it now; I just badly need to be with Dad and Scott. I can't take this crap without them.

I smother my emotions, hiding them from the world around me. I can feel them overwhelming me, causing anger to swelter. Pain, undeniable pain, turned my eyes red and my soul black. I am jealous of every living soul who has a mother to phone or hug. Damn you all.

I have been a lifelong fan of the TV show M.A.S.H. Both Natalie and I were raised on it; her by her grandfather, me by my parents. We love it so much that we have every episode on disc and watch it almost every night as we go to sleep. But I've found it extremely difficult to watch ever since Mom died. I don't know if it's that it reminds me of her or if it bothers me to laugh without her here. I think it's a bit of both. Anything that reminds me of her hurts. From her favorite TV shows to her favorite songs, each time I see or hear them it makes me cringe. I also find myself getting angry after I laugh. I'm sure it's trivial and will someday go away, but I hate the thought of ever being happy without her in my life. I've been through enough to know that time heals all wounds, but I can't imagine ever being happy or content with life without her in it. People always say that what doesn't kill you makes you stronger. Well, I should be one strong SOB after all this.

EXPLANATION: I found that a lot of things were hard to watch after Mom died. It seemed every time I turned on the television, Mom's favorite movies or shows were on. They were all painful reminders of the one person I would never see again.

CDU: Day 10
Woke up with Mom on the brain again; I just can't let go of the anger, frustration, and pain from her suicide. My dreaming of her didn't help much. I can't remember the specifics exactly, but I remember her being there and she was speaking to me. God, I miss her voice. Hell, I miss her totally and completely.

Scotty's thirty-fourth birthday is today; what do you give a guy who's lost so much in one month? A card won't suffice, and he's got enough money to buy anything he wants. Lord knows I don't. Either way; Scotty—if only I could bring Mom back.

A "normal" life, in my opinion, is now and forever unobtainable. When images of suicide, especially those of the one who brought you into this world, creep into your every thought and emotion, "normal" is nonexistent.

CDU: Day 11

I started this program strong, but I'm starting to not care again. I just want to get the program over with, so I can go on with my life. I've been thinking a lot about drinking lately. I guess I'm finally starting to get thirsty again. I know I don't need it, but God, do I ever want a drink. I have to stop this madness now. Natalie and Steven don't need this anymore; they've been through enough. Please God, help me stop. My life is so much better without that sewage. Please God, give me the strength to walk away from it now and forever.

EXPLANATION: When I started treatment I was hell-bent on the idea that I did not have a drinking problem. By the time I finished I realized the truth; I was an alcoholic. It was a tough pill to swallow, especially with everything else I was dealing with. As you'll read later, I just wish I would have stuck to this idea.

CDU: Day 12

My head is all over the place today. One second I'm high, then low, then ... lost. I've tried for the past twelve days to get something positive out of treatment; it's not happening! I understand to a point of why I was sent here but my primary problem is not alcohol, it's the fact that my mother shot herself. All this talk about alcohol and addiction is not getting me anywhere. I don't need a drink; I need my mother back. All these people and their propaganda and lies that they keep telling just to get out of here to have another drink is not affecting me one bit. The depression is what's killing me, not the alcohol. I've got to get the out of this place.

On day twelve of treatment our counselor led a discussion about what we would have to do in our lives to someday be "happy, joyous, and free." As normal, my thoughts etched themselves out on paper.

"Happy, joyous and free"
What a concept. Happy; I know I'll be happy again someday, my problem is believing in happiness. I often let Mom's suicide and my cravings for alcohol keep me from happiness. Mom never meant for me to be unhappy. She was hurting for years, and now she's not hurting anymore. I don't know if she's found happiness, but at least she's found some sort of peace. So eventually, I will find happiness even without Mom here. Alcohol, on the other hand, lies to me, making me think I'll be happier with it in my life. Lately the cravings have caused rough mood swings, which keep my happiness swaying like a ship in a storm. But eventually, through abstinence and sobriety, this too shall pass and I can regain my happiness.
What is joyous? I often think of it and happiness as the same thing. Or maybe joyous is being so happy that I can illuminate that to others around me. If that is joyous then I think it will take more time than just obtaining personal happiness. I feel I must tend to my own personal happiness before I can start projecting that happiness to others. Freedom is probably the one goal that I think I'll never achieve. I will always owe somebody something; I will never be able to just pick up and move every time I feel the need.
So happiness and joy I will someday attain, but I must accept that true freedom is nothing but a myth.

May 24, 2006

Dear Mom,

Just to let you know, I do not blame myself for your death. It's not my fault you did what you did. Everyone I've seen says at times I'll feel guilty, like if I would have called or lived closer you wouldn't have killed yourself. That's BS! I was, and remain a good son. I called most mornings after I got home just to check on you. I cared about you and loved you dearly and I know that you know that. So, like I said, I place no blame on myself.

Love,
Nelson

P.S. If I ever did anything to cause you pain or depression, I'm sorry.

EXPLANATION: My head was in so many different places during the first year after Mom's death. One second I'd be up, then down; overwhelmingly excited, and then totally depressed. I'd like to say that the medications I was on helped, but nothing did.

Insanity is my gift to myself. I crave insanity's nourishment to guide me further to self-destruction. Fear comforts me into a state of frozen numbness. I shun goodness just to stay in Lucifer's good graces. Hate is grateful, illustrious, and good. Oh, how I cleanse myself in sin's saturated filth. Woe is me; low is me; Hell I am in. I'm painted in violence, anger, aggression, and rage. Oh, how beautiful I must appear to no one.

EXPLANATION: Please understand, I have never and will never worship Satan or any other being other than the Lord, Jesus Christ. I looked back at my life, my history with alcohol use, and where I was with Mom's death and I began to put on paper what I saw from the insanity that surrounded me. This is my explanation that I came up with; this is how low my life had become.

Another book given to me my first few days at treatment was called *Daily Reflections*, which has a thought for each day of the week. I decided to sit down and write my thoughts on the topic from May 26, 2006.

"Turning negatives into positives"

I used to be good at this concept. Military life is full of negatives, but I've always been good at finding a better way to manage. Lately, I've had a hard time finding any positives in life. Minot doesn't help; Natalie and I really do hate this place. Our home life isn't bad, and Natalie likes her work. I guess if I really look at it, Nat and I just haven't tried to find anything positive around here. We just miss home so much. Mom's death made us realize just how much we need our families. But then I wonder if we would be any happier back in Texas? I wasn't in the best of all moods while we lived there, either. Am I just an unhappy person? I normally wouldn't think so but it looks as if I am. What in life would make me happy? How can I make a positive out of all my negatives?

1. *I need to remember that life could be worse.*
2. *I need to use my support systems more—Natalie, friends, Dad.*
3. *I need to remember the serenity prayer—and live it.*
4. *I need to remember that I can't change everybody else—I can only change my own attitude.*
5. *I need to simply walk away from situations that cause me stress.*
6. *I need to handle situations as they arise rather than put them off until it overwhelms me.*
7. *I need to pick one goal and not give up till that goal is accomplished.*
8. *I need to take at least thirty minutes per day for myself—quiet time, reading, meditation.*
9. *I need to exercise to help let go of some of this stress.*
10. *I need to remember that life will go on without Mom.*

EXPLANATION: All of these were great ideas; they would have truly helped if only I had stuck with them. I've always known the things to do to limit stress and anxiety in my life. But either I was too proud to admit I was stressed or too bull-headed to identify defeat. A person can have all the wisdom in the world; if they don't use it it does him or her any good.

My thoughts on the serenity prayer:
God, grant me the serenity to accept the things I
cannot change:

- *I can't change everyone around me. All I can do is accept that everyone else has to live with their problems and bad attitudes; I don't. Unless their actions or lack of actions are putting me or my family in harm's way, who gives a damn. If they want to surround themselves with stupidity, have fun. I can't change stupid.*

The courage to change the things I can:

- *One thing I know: I can change is me. I have to better myself for me and the family. If I can do something that impacts or changes things for the better in someone else's life, that's fine. But I've got to stop killing myself for those who couldn't care less. All I'm doing is wasting my time. Change me and let others deal with themselves, accordingly.*

And the wisdom to know the difference:

- *I've known the difference between right and wrong for years. Even though Mom went out the way she did she and Dad were excellent parents. I'm not the smartest guy in the world, but I'm wise enough to know that I am me and others are others. I might be able to inspire some but I can't affect all. I must tend to myself and my family and hope that others are wise enough to do the same.*

CDU: Day 15

It is a beautiful day today but not so much on the phone. Dad was having a rough morning. He's so upset with Mom's suicide. He told me that he obviously didn't love her enough. That's crap! Dad loved Mom, very much. This is one of those times that I'd love to punch Mom in her mouth. Why did she do this to us, especially Dad? Nine days after their thirty-five-year anniversary, she decided to swallow a bullet. How should Dad feel? I swear I will never understand this as long as I live.

God,
How can you make such a beautiful day during such a horrible time? I love Mom, and at the same time I hate her. Damn … I can't find the words.

Each night during treatment we were assigned homework; Day 15's assignment was to write about what we were thankful for. The following was my answer: (As you'll see I went quite a bit overboard.)

What am I thankful for?
I am thankful ...

- *to be 29 days sober.*

- *to still have one parent left—a father who is strong and able to see hope through the storm.*

- *for a loving wife who not only supports me through Mom's death, but who put up with all my years of alcohol dependency.*

- *for having a beautiful son, who reminds me that there is so much more to live for.*

- *to have other family members who I can call and at least know they're still alive.*

- *for my new friends I've met in treatment, who remind me that I'm not alone.*

- *for knowing who my higher power is and knowing that through prayer I can ask for his forgiveness, his strength, and his guidance through rough days.*

- *for windows in heaven, which Mom can look through and see that her guidance through our raising has paid off.*

- *for my parents who raised me to realize the difference between right and wrong, stupidity and wisdom.*

- *for those who have supported me, even when I was too drunk to realize it.*

- *for every morning I get to wake up to a new day, even if I don't want to.*

- *for every day filled with sunshine and every night filled with stars.*

- *for pictures which help remind me just how beautiful my mother was.*

- *for the thirty wonderful years I had with my precious mother.*

- *for each phone call I get from Dad and each comforting word he gives.*

- *for comforting hugs from my wife while my chest is quivering uncontrollably from crying too hard.*

- *for every time my son asks for a hot dog or a juice box.*

- *for every time my son kicks me in the head while we are sleeping; for every time he gives me a kiss before sleep; and for every time we say prayers at that time.*

- *for every time my son hears a fire truck siren and says it's Daddy's fire truck.*

- *for another day of sobriety and another day of sanity.*

I am thankful for so many more things but there's not enough paper in the notebook or ink in the pen.

EXPLANATION: I found it extremely important to add this to the book. Humans tend to focus on the negative even during mundane, trivial, everyday life. But negativity seems to overwhelm everything during difficult times. It's important to stop during times of great stress to remember those things that we can be thankful for.

Saturday, June 3, 2006: the first day out of CDU:
Wow, I can't explain how it feels to say I'm finished
with treatment. I never thought I'd be so proud to
say I am thirty-one days sober. Treatment helped me
more than I expected. I now realize that alcohol is
truly a problem for me. Plus, with all the depression
I still have ahead of me; I know that alcohol would
just make it worse. Either way, it's over. Now it's time
to return to the real world. Life … .bring it on!

Surprisingly, I actually had a hard time saying goodbye
to most of the people at the CDU. I made some pretty tight
bonds there, especially with the staff members.

Going into it, I expected to gain nothing out of this experience. However, what I found was that my like for alcohol
had drifted much farther to the love spectrum. I also found
that talking about both issues I was dealing with helped me
cope better with Mom's death. So, out of what I expected to
be a huge negative, I learned many positives.

NOTE: The following excerpts were written after I completed CDU, but due to their similarities, I felt it important
to include them as well.

Dear Mom,

Here comes another problem. I've realized since your passing that I get furiously scared when I can't get a hold of Natalie. Now, I'm so worried about losing those closest to me that I lose all self control when I can't reach them. Your loss destroyed me and I just don't think I could live with another loss again.

Sorry, but I'm too pissed to finish.

Nelson

Dear Mom,

Well, I'm officially blown away again. Natalie just reluctantly informed me that we're expecting our second child. I had all but given up on having another after your suicide because I didn't think it was fair to make another suffer through all of life's hell. And it really didn't help that she gave me this news today … the day before Father's Day; our first without you. How am I supposed to celebrate anything at this point? Hell, I barely want to exist at all. I just … can't.

I love you and miss you deeply.

Nelson

P.S. If we are going to have another, could you possibly ask God for us to have a baby girl? Natalie deserves a princess. Of course, a healthy baby is most important. Thanks.

Dear Mom,

I'm currently on a plane from Minneapolis to Dallas; going home to see the family, what's left of it. This will be the first time back home since you died. I have no clue what to expect once I walk back into that house. I'm hoping Dad chooses to start changing things up in there soon; it's not healthy for him to be trapped in so many memories. Dad said that the headstone will be finished in time for me to see it; I declined. So far I've been able to lie to myself about the reality of your death; if I see the headstone I won't be able to lie to myself any longer.

Oh, I miss you, Mom, so much. I found a picture of you and me that ripped me apart all over again. Yes, life itself, day to day is easier, but the pain creeps in when I least expect it. I am both happy and sad as you made home what it is.

Nelson

8 July, 06
Dear Mom,

Well, I survived my first official trip home with you not there. What a somber, dull building our house is now. What once was a wonderful place of love, joy, and happiness is now nothing more than a box of emptiness. My anger starts to set back in every time I see Dad because I imagine what hell he is in right now. I don't hate you for what you did, but I do hate what you did. No words will ever truly be able to express how much pain we all face every day. We will forever be covered in a cloak of destruction; one which you happily bestowed on us. I love you, but …

Nelson

EXPLANATION: The situation I was talking about here was nothing. Natalie had simply gone to the store to pick up groceries and left her cell phone at the house. Losing Mom so abruptly had terrified me of possibly losing someone else. It took months for me to lose that fear.

31 Dec, 06

Mom,

It's been a while since I've written, but I guess there could never be a better time; happy birthday. I would toast to you, being that it's also New Year's Eve but for some reason I can't quite find the motivation to celebrate. I guess your death kind of took the partying spirit away.

Our first Christmas without you was rough. I tried to put your memory out of my mind but it was easier said than done. Each time Steven opened a new gift I kept wondering what you would have sent him if you were still alive. The bigger his smile got, the more I wished you were there. He had a great Christmas; we all did. But one phone call was missing, the one with your voice on the other end of the line.

I have never been so happy and so hollow at the same time. Your absence from my life has emptied me out. I don't want to curse you anymore, yet I don't want to love you either.

God help me.

As hard as it was at times, putting my thoughts on paper put me at ease. It was my sounding board; my confidante. When I was experiencing things I thought no one else would understand, writing it down provided that release that I so desperately needed.

Mom at 100 Hooks Lodge showing off her big catch

My favorite picture of my mother and I.

14

The Fire Department Fiasco

After completing treatment and being away from work for over seven weeks, I knew that there would be many questions to answer, but I never expected what I walked into.

Firefighters are normally a very tight group committed to saving lives at all costs. To do this, you have to function as a team; no one man or woman can do it alone. Within that team there must be trust, and that's a concept that is earned over time. If something gets in the way of that trust or damages the relationships involved, it's very hard to regain it.

Returning just two weeks after Mom's death, there was no way I was ready to go back on the floor where I knew other's lives were dependent on me. I didn't even trust myself at the time. If you're not one hundred percent in this career field you can easily get people killed; I didn't want that on my conscience. So I got the help I needed, and I will never regret doing that. But in doing so, it erected barriers for which I was totally unprepared.

When a firefighter is identified as "mentally irregular," many flags are raised, especially if they have exhibited abnormal behaviors. You start to worry about their reliability to cover your back. Upper management knew everything that had happened related to Mom's suicide and my struggles thereafter. One of these individuals took it upon himself to bring everybody from my shift together to discuss the situation. This person walked into the room and stated, "You cannot talk about suicide, you cannot joke about suicide and anyone who does so will be severely reprimanded." He gave no further explanation as to why or from where his remarks had come. Making a comment like that and leaving it open to personal interpretation can stir up a ton of misconceptions. Everyone looked around the room, identified the one person that had been missing for a few weeks, and immediately stamped me as a suicide risk. Every bit of hard work and rapport I had built was thrown right out the window.

Luckily, explaining the situation to the military guys was not difficult at all. The civilians however, were a completely different story. It took one-on-one personal conversations and detailed explanations to even make a dent in rebuilding the trust factor. Eventually, I proved myself again; but this entire situation could have been completely avoided if one person would have simply considered the impact of his comments before making them public.

But once the truth was out, I had an entirely different problem to handle. Instead of seeking guidance and learning the best way to deal with me, everyone basically ignored me. I was already feeling alone in the world, so this only made things worse. I understand the idea of not throwing me back in the deep end without a life preserver; I wasn't ready for that yet. But to be shunned, to be ignored due to their ignorance or because they were afraid of offending me, that only intensified the issue.

NOTE: People who experience similar situations will be devastated, to say the least. It may take a great deal of time to get them back to the person they were before the incident happened. I'm not saying they have to have their hand held all the time, but ignoring or isolating them can have a very adverse effect.

Other members of management proved to be exactly what I needed them to be. One individual in particular ended up becoming like a brother to me. Master Sergeant Michael Wilkinson, now retired, became my voice of reason. He always did his best to make me feel comfortable and continually expressed his concern for me. He didn't look at me as a number or a spot to fill; he truly cared. He wasn't worried about my professional military bearing at the time but the whole person concept. He reminded me I was an asset and that, with time and patience, I would get back to the staff sergeant I was before.

One night while I was working a twenty-four-hour shift, Mike came around and asked how things were going on the home front. This was around the time that Dad and a new "friend," still to be introduced, were getting pretty serious. He allowed me to vent my emotions and frustrations for nearly thirty minutes without interruption.

Then he related a similar situation about his father who had remarried within three months of divorcing his mom. He told me about the confusion it brought to the family and the people who eventually turned against his father. Then Mike offered me a nugget of wisdom. He said that if he had known then what he knows now, it wouldn't have bothered him at all. In hindsight, he can see why his father decided to pick up and move on with his life. His parents had been married for over fifteen years. To go from being with someone that long to not having anyone to come home to has to be extremely difficult. Furthermore, he added that all the frustration and anger he felt toward his dad at that time now seems quite trivial.

Discussions like this with Mike really helped me cope with all the confusion surrounding me. He showed interest in the progression of my mental stability. Instead of just treating me as a subordinate, he treated me as a friend and brother ... the exact treatment I needed.

Another individual who helped considerably was Tech Sergeant Kenneth Kline. While we didn't have as many heart-to-heart conversations, Sgt. Kline helped in a completely different manner. Knowing me as he did, he knew the best way to keep my mind at ease was to keep me working and involved in things I cared about. Sgt. Kline gave me projects and jobs to pique my interests which, in turn, kept me level-headed. He took the time to ensure I was coping well, both at work and at home. He kept a close watch on me and intervened when he saw I might be approaching a danger zone. He and his wife provided the support and guidance needed to help both me and my family past the most trying time of our lives.

I've always differentiated the good from the bad. I learn lessons from mistakes, both mine and others', and take note where I see great things done. While some things from this experience I will definitely chalk up as what not to do, I also gained great friends and appreciation for their efforts.

NOTE: Whether you are a manager, friend, family member, or bystander, take the time to let people know you care. Be there for them with a listening ear and a sympathetic heart. And if you are the victim of a tragic event, I hope and pray that among all your connections you have a "Mike Wilkinson" or "Kenneth Kline" to lend the advice, support and friendship you need to make it through.

15

What I Refused to Be

𝆑

Three months into my rebuilding process, a woman stopped me after a meeting we had attended. She introduced herself, quickly apologized for the hell I had been going through, and reminded me there were better days to come. She appeared to be in her mid to late thirties, and would best be described by my father in his southern lingo as someone who had been "rode hard and put up wet." Her clothes were badly wrinkled, her eyes were droopy and shadowed by black bags, and her overall expression resembled a fighter who had just gone twelve rounds with Ali. It seemed whatever demons she was battling were winning.

Having never met this lady before, and trying to be polite, I hesitatingly dabbled in small talk to find out what she needed. What I expected to be a simple conversation between two struggling addicts became a slap in the face I'd never forget.

She began to tell me a story of a friend who had purposely overdosed on drugs. She spoke about how close they had been and how he had introduced her to the world of drug addiction. She broke down as she described how her life eventually spiraled out of control and how the loss had increased her drug usage to the point that she had attended twelve different treatment facilities, most due to court order.

The more she spoke, the worse I felt. But it was her final words that sent chills down my spine. In an effort to be encouraging, she promised things would someday get better and that brighter days were soon to come.

"Brighter days?" I thought to myself. If she was having "brighter days," I'd hate to see what bad ones brought with them. Here was a woman who had basically shot up, smoked, or snorted her life away over a friend's suicide. Obviously "brighter days" were evading her at every turn.

I apologized to her for the loss of her friend and asked how long ago it had happened.

"Sixteen years ago," she replied.

Hold up a minute! Sixteen years? Hell no! No way was I going to allow the death of anyone to devastate me to the point that my life would ever basically cease to exist! Not a chance. Yes, Mom's death was beyond the point of painful to a level I will never fully be able to describe using any worldly language. But I refuse to let it turn me inside out; I refuse.

I left there feeling destroyed all over again. But as I drove away I started to understand the significance of our meeting. I can't speak for others' resolve and their ability to bounce back after a life altering situation. I can pray and hope the best for them, but ultimately it is up to them to decide. Our conversation made me see clearly that I, through the assistance of God, am in control of my personal resolve. I make the decision of whether Mom's death would be a hurdle or an unraveling of life.

From that moment I decided I would not allow myself to fall apart that way. I knew it wasn't going to be an immediate fix and that getting over the initial affects of mom's suicide would be my toughest personal struggle to date. But no matter how difficult it would be and how many obstacles manifested themselves during the journey, I'd make it though; I'd survive it.

From that point on, I set a list of personal goals:

- Grieve for no more than a year
- Start the healing process once I'm done grieving, no sooner
- Within a year and a half start to transform the pain into something worthwhile
- Ensure that the family heals and stays together

I never saw that lady again but I hope and pray that somehow she finds peace within the storm.

NOTE: Please understand, everyone deals and heals with tragedy in his or her own way; but there's one main point to remember. To accomplish any goal in life one must have the determination to succeed no matter what it takes. If life knocks you down; get up, brush yourself off, learn from your mistakes, and start swinging back.

16

Minot

Minot, North Dakota, is simply a place that you either love or love to hate. For those within the deemed "Magic City," most residents are extremely proud of their small town. I cannot say whether I love it or hate it; however, I can say that our first year was extremely difficult, which, in turn, made Minot seem like a very dreary place.

NOTE: The following excerpts were written within the first three months after mom's death. Please understand that following such a destructive experience, any place would seem horrible.

Who in the hell would choose to live in this blasted state? I've worked in freezers that were warmer than this hell hole. How am I supposed to fight depression when you can't see the sun for six months at a time? What a wasteland. If the depression doesn't kill me, this place may take its claim instead.

If Hell ever froze over, I imagine its settings to appear much like Minot, North Dakota. What a dreadful place, this Minot—so cold, so desolate, so dreary. It's the only place I've ever seen where the sun, in all its power and eminence, is relentlessly choked to sheer lifelessness. Its bitter cold clinches so tight that breath refuses to exhale. Hellacious winds rip through clothing layers like they're nonexistent. Joy is a mere fairytale in this valley of gloom. Depression is the only state of mind in this town, the fabled "the Magic City."

Pain, suffering, anguish, and depression are all that I feel. I'm a soul lost at sea with no compass or oar. Devastation is all I feel, that and the agonizing cold of this bitter place of despair. Warmth is but a myth in a frozen wilderness of flat hills and desolate forests. I suffocate in the blinding grayness of a sky with no color and a peace with no hope. I try to take a new step but find myself frozen to the ground. I've got to free myself from this state and state of mind.

16 December 2008
This is it, the last night. Three years in this hell, this frozen tundra, this barren wasteland. The last night in the place where I lost her, lost myself, and found my purpose. I let it go; all of it. The pain, the suffering, the fear of the dark, I leave it all behind me on that final exit. I leave with pride, dignity, and what's left of my sanity. The new addition of our daughter to the family helped; yet merely covered the wound. All we've longed for is to leave; to flee the destination which has haunted us. Now we have that; an end. I pray for the new. I pray for the future abroad. I pray for peace within us.

We were forced to return home four times during our first year in Minot, either for deaths in the family or personal issues. As a family, we always do our best to make good out of any situation. But after three years and far too many deaths and hardships in the family, we had simply had enough.

Minot is truly a great town with many wonderful people residing there. It wasn't that Minot was a bad place, but simply that so many ill things happened while we were there that even the prettiest of areas would have seemed like a living hell. I seriously feel that we could have lived in such a place as Hawaii or Florida; with all the situations we had, those too would have been hell to live in. Though certain situations I experienced while living there were excruciating; they are a part of the past. I now look upon your town fondly. The time when I wrote these inserts was a very difficult one; however, that is the past. I now look upon your town fondly.

17

A Slap of Reality

🖋

For the majority of the eight months following Mom's death, I felt nothing but rage towards her. Mom, for a reason only she knew, felt her situation was so terrible that she made the most drastic of decisions possible. If she and Dad had been having problems, she could have divorced him. If she was having mental issues, she could have sought treatment. But instead, she took the one way out that was easiest for her, and the toughest on those of us left behind. I didn't care what her reason was; the blame fell where the gun did. This notion built a huge fire in me, and I had no problem letting it be known. I used every word imaginable to describe her and my feelings toward her. I literally hated her during that time for leaving us.

Society has a way of destroying all the good a person has done by inflating the significance of one wrongdoing; I was following the exact same pattern toward my mother. I ignored the significance of thirty wonderful years and focused on the fact that she left the way she did. Yes, her means were extreme and destroyed the foundation my family had been built on, but by replacing her existence with hate I was forgetting all the wonderful things she had done. I verbally bashed her, no matter who was in the nearby vicinity. I wore my anger like a cloak, prevalent enough for all to see. A friend saw this, and slapped me back into reality.

During one of my tirades, I made the comment that I was

better off without my mother since she was so selfish anyway. Daniel Miller, the friend who was by my side the night Mom died, whirled me around like I was a feather, forcefully slamming me against a wall. Confused and taken back, I quickly learned what caused his actions. "I'm sick of you talking shit about your mother," he yelled. "Before, all you could do was praise your Mom, but now that she's dead you can't stop trashing her. You're being a bitch about all of this. Yes, she's dead; but if she meant anything to you in life she should mean ten times more now that she's gone."

After some moments passed, Dan released his death grip and reminded me that no matter how much I hated her and how much I despised her actions, it would never bring her back. Eventually I would have to make the decision to either let go of the hate or eternally ignore the love I had always felt for my mother. He showed me how childishly I was reacting to her death. Most importantly, he reminded me of the little ears that were hearing every word from my mouth, those of my son. Someday, I would have to answer to him for what had happened to his grandmother and that I would always want him to remember the goodness she possessed.

I'm extremely lucky that Dan, a former Marine who possessed the ability to twist me in to a pretzel, didn't follow through with it. But mostly, I'm grateful that Dan was a true friend and showed me the error of my ways. I'm grateful that he stopped me from trashing the image of such a beautiful mother even more than I already had. And overall, I'm just grateful that he was a friend when I truly need it.

Thanks Dan.

8 Jan, 2007
Dear Mom,

It's been a while since I've written you. Life has gotten a lot better since then. I'm now very sorry for all the angry words I said about you and to you. It took a good friend to make me realize how wrong I was. I still love you just like always and I miss you, oh so much.

Nelson

18

Jostacia

It was the night before Fathers Day, 2006. All day, I could tell Natalie had something on her mind. I figured she had a big surprise for me and was just anxious to unveil it. Was I ever right!

I was sitting in bed watching TV when Natalie came in, laid down beside me, and started making casual conversation. After about three minutes of basic small talk, she said, "Well, happy Father's Day again." This seemed completely out of the blue being that it was still the night before Father's Day and this was her first mention of it. I replied thank you but questioned the raw announcement and its timing. Her reply, "Well, I figured since you're about to be a father again I would just say happy Father's Day."

I was immediately flabbergasted, decimated, and overwhelmed! This was the last thing I expected or ever wanted to hear Natalie say. My decision was made the day Mom died; no more kids, period! I couldn't fathom bringing another child into the world. It was bad enough that I would have to explain to Steven what had happened to his "Me-maw" ; I'll be damned if I wanted to do it twice!

But it was out of my hands at that point. Knowing Natalie, she would have had it checked, rechecked, and triple checked before making that announcement to me. We had already had the discussion about not having another child and due to that I could tell her reluctance to inform me at all.

I could also see the disappointment in her eyes with my lack of enthusiasm. But what did she expect? I had already made my thoughts on the idea perfectly clear and now was being faced with the direct opposite. I wanted to be excited, but I just didn't have it in me.

My lack of enthusiasm continued the entire nine months of Natalie's pregnancy. I tried with everything in me to be happy, but Mom's passing had stolen that and left me void of any excitement … even the approaching birth of our second child. This put untold stress and strain on Natalie. She knew I was still devastated by Mom's suicide, and she did her best to support me, yet she received little in return. All she wanted was for me to be happy about the new addition.

I played the game as well as I could. I prepped and painted a new room for our expected baby girl. I did the whole daddy ritual of buying clothes and helping to pick out baby furniture; still nothing. Nothing could get me excited about becoming a father again, which in turn, made me feel even worse. No matter what I tried, I could not find my joy.

6 Feb, 07
Dear Mom,

Good Lord willing, your granddaughter will be born today.

This has been a pretty difficult load to bear. I've had a hard time getting excited about a new addition to the family. How the hell am I supposed to get excited about an event I never wanted to happen? Right after your suicide, Nat and I agreed not to force another child to have to suffer life's anguish. We already felt bad that Steven would someday feel the pain that life can dish out. Why would we subject another child to such torment? So, of course, it was a complete shocker when just a short month later we found out we were pregnant. Since then, I've struggled daily to find the joy about becoming a daddy again. I want so badly to be excited with Nat about the baby but I can't. How can I get excited about a new life when the majority of the time I don't even want mine? Damn it Mom, what is the point to all this? You chose to take your life then God sends a new one our way. I'm hoping that all this passes once I see her; if not, I have no clue how I'm going to be a father to a child I don't want. If you're near God right now please ask him to send me some love ... scratch that; I'd just throw it away. Damn, I'm going to go, Mom. The doctor is about to induce Nat.

What am I going to do?

Shortly after I wrote this excerpt I realized God must have been listening. On February 6, 2007, my life started over again when I looked into the eyes of my newborn baby girl. Jostacia Brilynn Thomas became my pride and joy from the second she graced us with her presence. All the worry and strife that had built up was flushed away in a glance. She was beautiful, and her existence filled the void created on 17 April, 2006. Jostacia reminded me that it was okay to be happy again even without Mom being in my life. She was, is, and always will be Daddy's little princess.

19

A Splitting of the Family

Mom's death created a huge wedge between Scotty and Dad who, up till then, had always been extremely close. Dad started to date fairly quickly after the loss: within three weeks to be exact, and this enraged Scotty. I was fine with it at first but, impressionable as I was at the time, just one conversation with Scotty made me do a complete 180.

Right after Mom's death, Dad made some promises to Scotty and I, the most important of those was to not make any major changes for the first year. Scotty and I both felt this would be best and tried to hold him to it; however, Dad changed his mind shortly after.

Within a few months, Dad started speaking quite often about a woman named Vickie. He knew her through church and had been quite close with her parents for years. At first, I figured a simple friendship would be a good thing for him. But "simple" quickly turned into a serious relationship, and with it followed discussions of major changes, including the selling of the house. Needless to say, Scotty and I didn't take to the idea very well, and it drove a huge wedge between Dad and Scotty. I did my best to support Dad, but the redirection from his promises bothered me something fierce.

In regards to Vickie, at least for my sake, it didn't have anything to do with her as a person because in all honesty she is a complete sweetheart. The presence of another woman wasn't what bothered us. It was just way too soon in our estimation, and it simply wasn't Mom. Dad could have brought home Mother Teresa and again, it still wouldn't be Mom. Vickie took quite a few blows simply because the one woman we saw best for dad had left and left us mortally wounded.

Looking back on it now, I understand why Dad tried to move on and rebuild his life. Mom and Dad had been together for thirty-five years; a marriage of that duration makes it difficult being single again. Furthermore, I admire Vickie for who she is and for being there for him during such a devastating period. But as I said, the timing just didn't seem right for Scotty and me.

The battle between Scotty and Dad really ate me up inside. I wanted to support both of them, to be there for them despite their personal feelings. Scotty exhibited nothing but anger at the situation. Dad, on the other hand, just wanted us to accept Vickie and understand his need to press on with life. I felt like a human ping-pong ball. I was so mixed up with my own feelings and too afraid to offend either of them by telling them that I didn't agree that I simply became a "yes man." "Yes, Pop, you should move on with your life." "You're right, Scotty, Pop isn't showing proper respect to Mom for moving on so fast." Somehow, I had become the biggest ass-kisser I've ever known. If I had the opportunity to go back in time, I would literally kick my own ass. Neither Scotty nor Dad needed a yes man; they needed guidance. Of course I was the last man to give guidance, but support—I could have handled that. The truth was that I was so angry at Mom during that period that I did think Dad should move on, just to spite her. The fact was that if she hadn't made the decision or performed the action that she had, none of us would have to make any changes at all.

NOTE: In society, even if death is ruled a suicide, someone usually takes the blame or gets ruled as the "reason." Those people closest to the one who committed suicide inevitably become the "bad guy" or one who should have caught the signs. Unfortunately, until innocence is proven beyond the shadow of a doubt that person is presumed guilty.

Dad obviously took the hit on this one. I never wanted to blame Dad, but like so many others, I felt I had to blame somebody. In mine and most others' minds, Mom was too sweet, innocent, and kind to have pulled that trigger. Someone must have forced her hand.

It didn't help that others kept questioning if Dad had something to do with it. I tried my best not to speculate on the subject, but when Mom's side of the family and a few others continually pushed the idea, it was hard to ignore. I finally came to the conclusion, through some investigative fact finding, that Dad didn't have anything to do with Mom's death. In other words, I know that Mom killed herself on her own terms and for reasons that will forever remain known only to her.

The battle between Scotty and Dad quickly became the battle between Scotty and me versus Dad. During the 2006 Christmas holiday, dad had flown up to North Dakota to spend time with Nat, Steven, and myself. When he told us he was coming, I knew he and Vickie had decided to get married. I figured he wanted to break the news to me before it hit Scotty's doorstep.

Sure enough, after dinner one night he asked me and Natalie for our opinions on the subject. Without needing a mirror, I knew the expression on my face was not the one he wanted. I don't know if he expected me and Natalie to jump for joy and throw a party, but it didn't happen. He had promised to wait a year before making any major decisions or changes; that promise had just been broken. Worse than that, he had decided to give us this news just a few days before the first Christmas without Mom. Obviously, Mom was the last thing on his mind.

Not surprised at Dad's news, I reminded him of his promises to Scotty and me. His response was immediate ... we had our families and he deserved the chance to have one, too. Frustrated, I simply told him to do what he felt best because he hadn't listened to us anyway. He countered by trying to paint her as the epitome of human beings, which was totally unnecessary. We had already met her and had a pretty decent impression of her.

But the conversation quickly spiraled downward with his next line of reasoning. He told us issues Mom was experiencing before she died and conversations they'd had during that time. He painted a dark picture of a woman who had grown bitter toward her own grandkids. But he truly crossed the line when he said, "To be honest, Vickie will probably love your kids better than your mother did."

This is where I wish we had one of those sound panels attached to the side of the book where you could push a button to hear tires screeching to a halt. It took a fraction of a second for my temper to go through the roof; I was livid! It took every ounce of my being to not make myself an orphan in that instant. One quick glance at Natalie revealed obvious worry as to how I would react. Mustering all the restraint at my disposal, I glared at him and growled out the only word I dared. "Don't." There were a million other words fighting to take aim at him, but "don't" was the only one I allowed myself.

Pushing back from the table, I left the room in dead silence. As I took the stairs to our room, each step came with mounting fury and frustration. What could he have possibly hoped to accomplish by making a comparison like that? It was asinine. Every emotion I had felt since Mom's death came rushing back in tidal waves of anger, rage, fear, and threats of insanity. I simply could not believe he had crossed that line!

After some time, I was finally able to regain my composure. Reluctantly making my way down stairs, I turned the corner to find my wife wiping tears from her eyes. My father, realizing he was a long way from home in an extremely cold place, remained silent. With clinched fists, I took a deep breath and looking him straight in the eye made a promise. "If you ever want to see this family again, you'll bite your tongue the next time you want to make a comment like that." Being the father he is and knowing he had just made one of the worst mistakes of his life, he tried to apologize. It was too late, the damage was irreparably done.

NOTE: A word to the wise for any spouse that may be left behind: never make disparaging comments or unfavorable comparisons of the deceased. Enough said.

Once Scotty heard of this conversation and the lack of respect shown to Mom, he went ballistic. The relationship between him and Dad virtually evaporated. For the next year, their relationship consisted of Dad calling and talking solely to Megan. Scotty literally wanted nothing to do with him.

I chalked dad's comment up to momentary stupidity and have let it go for the most part. After all, he is the only parent I have left, and the only grandparent still living on my side of the family for my kids. Scotty simply added it in with all the other barriers between the two of them.

This antagonistic struggle lasted the better part of four years. Dad kept trying to get Scotty to open up to him with little success. There was casual conversation from time to time, but it never lasted long. A short, two-day visit with an occasional game or two of cards was about the extent of their relationship.

I can't speak for Scotty on his ill temperament toward dad. Maybe there's more to the story than I've been let in on; I don't know. All I do know is that Scotty and Dad used to be very close. That all disintegrated the moment that gun fired. Things will never be the way they were between the two of them, ever. All I can hope for is peace and a possible truce somewhere in the future.

NOTE: Once an event like this happens, normal becomes a figment of your imagination. Family dynamics change; expect it. Be willing to adapt or life will go on without you! Looking back, I have learned there is no right way to deal with the turmoil left after a suicide. The only advice I can give is leave yourself options; don't make a decision that is set in stone. Leave yourself outs so if you identify that you made a bad choice, you have an easier time of transitioning out of the situation.

20

Church

L ike most people that lose a friend or family member tragically, I too experienced a period of deep anger towards God. I questioned him as to why someone so beautiful and loving would do such a desperate and despicable act. I hated Him for not being there when she needed Him most. I continually asked why ... only to find no answer in return.

But once the initial shock wore off, I found that I wasn't upset with God at all. I have always believed that God works in mysterious ways and that we'll never truly understand His purpose behind certain things in life. Even though I didn't understand why she died the way she did, I never stopped believing or loving Him.

My anger and disappointment was quickly directed at the church that my family had attended for years. Now, I know that there is great deliberation between the true meaning of church, but I was always raised and still believe that church is an assembly of people who gather and give praise to God. I believe it should be centered on love and acceptance. I was raised in a certain denomination of church which was always taught to me and my brother as being "the right church." I found that particularly eyebrow-raising in that I never found the part in the Bible which annotated the "right church" among all the "wrong churches." However, I went along with the charade until I was old enough to make my own choices and seek refuge elsewhere.

A few months before my mother died she and I had a discussion about the "church" and why I had faded so far out of its existence. When I told her of my issues she opened up about some personal concerns of her own that I had never known. We journeyed back through our family's history with a certain congregation, and she expressed to me some very troublesome thoughts that she had concerning past situations and the way our family was treated by a number of fellow members. She went further to say that the congregation had grown to be more of a political cage fight rather than a sanctuary.

One comment she said stuck with me in that she stated "why can't we simply come together, praise the Lord, and love one another." It's ironic; I always thought that was the point behind church as well.

Further ideas were brought out in the discussion; however, it's best that I keep those exploits between my mother and me. Either way, the entire discussion left me with an overall feeling of her dissatisfaction and pent-up confusion.

My mother was a servant to everyone. She very rarely had a bad thing to say about anyone and always did her best to see the good in others. However, one frailty my mother did have is that she was very naïve and somewhat emotionally dependent on others. She needed to be able to help others and do things for them. She didn't necessarily need anything in return, a simple smile was enough. But when she found that the one place in her life where she should have been able to receive smiles and to take care of others eventually slammed the door in her face; she was heartbroken. Everyone became so caught up in their own personal agendas that they forgot the single most important aspect behind church ... love.

Do I blame the church solely for the death of my mother? No. But I do know that the one place she should have been able to find mercy, forgot what mercy was.

I know that someone reading this will scream that it's not the church that grants mercy, and that it didn't seem like her faith was in the right place. But before you cast the first stone let me ask, "Is it not the members of a church who are supposed to make everyone feel welcome?"

NOTE: This chapter is not intended to offend anyone or put down the establishment of church. I have been to many churches in my life and have met some wonderful people whose sole purpose is to praise God and love others. However, I do stand by the idea that people are not to pass judgment on others when it comes to salvation and condemnation. God judges. There are enough problems and issues here on earth for us to contend with; passing judgment and placing ourselves above others is not one of those. I do not believe that any church congregation is better than another. As humans we must study and interpret the word of God and build a personal relationship with him. I do believe in the importance of meeting with fellow believers. But I do not believe that a church, or members of any church, has the right or power to pass divine judgment.

- *Colossians 3:12 says so, as those who have been chosen of God, holy and beloved, put on a heart of compassion, kindness, humility, gentleness and patience;*

- *Ephesians 4:32 tells us to be kind to one another, tender-hearted, forgiving each other, just as God in Christ also has forgiven you.*

- *2 Corinthians 5:10 reminds us that we must all appear before the judgment seat of Christ, so that each one may be recompensed for his deeds in the body, according to what he has done, whether good or bad.*

- *Finally, Romans 14:10-11 asks why do you judge your brother? Or you again, why do you regard your brother with contempt? For we will all stand before the judgment seat of God. For it is written,*

"AS I LIVE, SAYS THE LORD, EVERY KNEE SHALL BOW TO ME, AND EVERY TONGUE SHALL GIVE PRAISE TO GOD."

21

When You Know You've Had a Rough Time

It was May of 2007 and I was ten days away from heading to a military educator's course in Montgomery, Alabama. I had successfully passed the one-year mark after Mom's death and had also lasted a full year without alcohol. I was proud of how far I had come.

Even though things had been looking up for me I had been feeling mysteriously under the weather the past few weeks. It started with a decrease in energy, followed by spells of dizziness. Shortly I found myself becoming extremely exhausted after climbing a single flight of stairs. Next came several bouts with nausea and vomiting. But the final straw was a severe case of dizziness, nausea, vomiting, and a blackout while mowing the yard.

My wife decided that she had seen enough, put me in the car, and drove me to the emergency room. There I spent the next four hours getting stuck, poked, prodded, and ex-rayed. After hours of boredom and continual waiting, a doctor came into the room and informed us that he had bad news and possible worse news.

The doctor suggested that with all the symptoms I was having and a look at my lung x-rays, it was possible I had a severe case of walking pneumonia. Knowing that walking pneumonia was nothing to play around with, we assumed the doctor had started with the worst scenario. But then he said, "And now to the possible worse news." Natalie and I took a quick glance at each other and swallowed hard in preparation for what was about to come.

He started by pulling two x-ray slides from a folder and fastening them on the viewer. The first he identified as a view of my heart taken a year before, and the second as one they had taken that day. There was a significant increase in the size of my heart in a year's time, which could indicate a condition that was weakening the heart walls. He was concerned that further swelling could cause my heart to rupture, in which case a possible heart transplant would be in my future.

There was total silence as I tried to understand the impact of his words. I looked at Natalie for a full ten seconds before we both erupted into gales of laughter. Totally bewildered and somewhat curt the doctor asked, "Did I miss something?" Natalie quickly explained the majority of what had happened within the year prior and that with the way our luck was going this just followed smoothly in succession. Unable to see the humor, the doctor shook his head and left the room.

In our relief, after an extreme amount of tests and screenings, I was diagnosed with walking pneumonia and given proper treatment and prescriptions to rid me of the illness. Yes, we understood the gravity of the situation, but there's nothing to do sometimes after a continual dosage of bad days but laugh it off and move on.

22

Chris Benoit

It was the morning of June 26, 2007. I was all set to graduate from a five-week professional military educator's course on the Gunter Annex of Maxwell Air Force Base in Montgomery, Alabama. My regular morning ritual was thrown out the window to preparing for the final exam. My car was gassed, packed, and ready for me to start the seventeen-hour trek to Dallas, Texas, as soon as the instructors called "class dismissed." This was the first time I had been separated from my wife and children for longer than a week, and I was almost desperate to see their beautiful faces.

Feeling a little apprehensive about the pending test, I was nonetheless ready to finish yet another demanding military education course. The past five weeks had been spent developing camaraderie among the classmates. Now being a diehard fan of professional wrestling since childhood, I invited everyone to my room to watch either Raw or Smack Down from the WWE every Monday and Friday night. Most nights I'd watch TV alone, but at least the offer was there.

I was unable to catch the airing of Raw the previous night since I was preparing for both the test and the trip.

The next morning, I strolled into the PME (Professional Military Education) building with both anxiety and anticipation weighing heavily. Questions immediately started flying my way as soon as I entered the classroom. "How are you?" Are you okay?" Puzzled by all the concern, I soon learned a professional wrestler had killed his family and himself the day prior. No one could remember the name of the deceased wrestler so I quickly headed for the media center to research the details. Panic mounted as I waited for the computer to connect to Fox news.com, worried about what I might find. And then, there it was. "Wrestler Murders Family; Commits Suicide." My heart sank to my stomach as I recognized the picture of Chris Benoit. The more I read, the more distressed I became.

Popular or not, I have been captivated by the sport of professional wrestling my whole life. Of the thousands of performers I had watched, none had impressed me more than Chris Benoit. Chris's style of wrestling and his charisma had made him my favorite for years. Although he wasn't the largest or most popular by the fans, he simply worked his butt off, and I loved him for it. From every match I had recorded of him, to his personal DVD which told his life story, I could just see that he had a strong work ethic. It didn't matter what he had to do to accomplish something, he would do it and do it better than anyone else could. I truly admired the guy.

As soon as I saw his picture, it was like someone slapped me square in the face. Everything from Mom's suicide came racing back at me: all the "whys", the pain, the sorrow; everything in one swift instant. Added to that was the horrifying fact that not only had he killed himself but also his wife and son. I couldn't fathom it.

The rest of the morning played itself out like a nightmare. I went through the motions of taking the test and graduating without mental application whatsoever. I could not concentrate on anything other than the horrific facts of the deaths. The familiar ache in my chest returned. The same questions, the same emotional instability, the same numbness. Comprehension was simply beyond my grasp. A little more than a year after Mom's suicide I felt devastated all over again.

Now you may be asking yourself why this was such a big deal to me. Well, most of us find that one hero, figure, or celebrity who just captivates us. Chris Benoit did that for me. Many people think wrestling is stupid, but wrestlers put themselves on the line everyday in the name of entertainment. It's like a huge action movie, only with a continuing storyline. And I had followed Chris Benoit for so many years; I seriously had built him up as the person I wanted to mirror. With every assault or move he enacted the intensity showed in his face. Now he was gone and all I could see was that I had basically lost two heroes to the same fate.

Somehow I passed my test and made it through graduation, then pointed my car toward Texas. I called my wife and briefly discussed Chris's death and its effects on me. She expressed her concerns and asked if I wanted to stay another night at the base to calm down for the trip. I couldn't; I needed to see my family, badly. I told her I would be okay and that I'd call as soon as I was out of Alabama.

I started my car and looked at myself in the mirror. A huge rush of anxiety hit me like a typhoon and I remember feeling as if the walls of the car were closing in on me. I was suffocating in fear, the fear of never seeing my wife and children again. I tried to focus solely on driving and getting to Texas as I pulled the car out of the parking lot and headed toward the back gate. Pulling onto the interstate, I remember feeling like I was locked in a casket, pushing forward to my imminent death. I kept seeing flashes of my car running off the road and hitting trucks, embankments, or anything else large enough to do severe damage. It was almost as if I was literally fighting a battle within myself where my right hand was trying to pull the wheel toward something to hit as the left hand was trying to keep the car straight. A part of me was trying to die while the other was fighting to survive.

After fighting the mental battle for half an hour, I realized there was no way I was going to be able to continue and make it all the way to Texas. I grabbed my cell phone and called Natalie. Knowing my background and the respect I had for Chris Benoit, she was not surprised of the severe effects on me. When I told her about the flashes I was having she told me to pull the car over and take a break. We talked about fifteen minutes while Natalie did her best to calm me down. The flashes had ceased, but the huge weight of anxiety was crushing my chest, causing intense pain. Natalie suggested I get a room for the night, but I knew the urges would return. I also knew without anyone to talk me through it, there was a good chance they would win. The one person I knew could help me was Marvin Williams. Throughout the five-week class, Marvin and I had spoken a lot about Mom and the effect it had on my life for the past year. Besides just being my instructor, he had become a very good friend. Natalie agreed it would probably be best for me to return to Gunter.

Making an about face, I headed back toward base. In route, I called Marvin on his cell phone and gave him a heads up about what was happening. The return trip was like an out-of-body experience; I had to talk myself through each move. I remember fighting to keep my concentration off Chris Benoit and Mom and more on getting back to Gunter. The flashes returned, but they were different. I saw flashing images of Chris and graphic visuals from the night before. What had happened? How could a lifelong hero become such a villain overnight? How could a man I had idolized for so long become a murderer of his own wife and son? The questions kept tearing through my mind again and again.

Somehow, in spite of all the whirling thoughts in my brain, I made it back to Gunter. Mark was waiting for me at the door; I could see he was scared for me. We sat in his office for an hour as I explained what happened that morning. He had heard about the murder/suicide and knew I was a huge wrestling fan, but had not put the two together. He suggested that I speak to his squadron's first sergeant and a chaplain.

He also asked me if I would have any problems speaking with a counselor who was a personal friend. At that point, I was desperate and reaching out for any answers I could get, so I agreed.

Throughout the day I spoke with the three individuals explaining all the stresses experienced over the past year. Then I explained how the news of Chris Benoit had brought all those feelings and more crashing back on me.

The first sergeant and chaplain helped to put me at ease, but it was the counselor that really brought it all home for me. Up to that point, I didn't see the connection. Chris was someone I had never met; a man I only knew through watching TV. Yet three decisions he had made in his life turned mine upside down. Since Mom's death I had heard of countless suicides and murders, yet none of them had affected me in this way. Why was this one so different?

The counselor helped me to dissect the situation. She asked me how long I had been watching Chris Benoit on TV and what interested me about him. I replied that he had been my favorite wrestler for almost fifteen years and that I had basically mirrored my work ethics off of what I had seen from him in the ring. I explained to her that even though most people around me thought it was childish, Chris had become something of an icon to me.

The counselor asked if I had any memorabilia of his over the past fifteen years. My answer: Only thirty to fifty recordings of his matches, with my favorite disc being a documentary of his life inside and outside of the ring. Furthermore, my son has several toys of his and I had no clue how I would someday explain Chris' demise.

It took the counselor a matter of seconds to connect the dots. She explained that the grieving process from a suicide within the family can take years to overcome and that my-year long struggle put me still in the early stages. She could see how much I truly admired my mother and how much pain it caused me by the way I spoke of her. Children who have a very tight bond with their parents idolize them and basically look at them as heroes. Mom's actions had affected me so horribly that I had felt betrayed by my idol, my hero.

Then the talk reverted to Chris Benoit and how the recent events had sent me into such a tail spin. She explained that we watch sports stars or wrestlers in these heroic battles for years and learn so much from them and about them that we feel like we know them personally. In my case, I had followed the personal life and professional career of Chris Benoit so adamantly and so intensely that I began to idolize him, making him a hero. It didn't matter that I had never personally met him. Just watching him week after week, episode after episode, for fifteen years formed a bond much like the one I had with my mother. And now that he had chosen the same path as she, taking his own wife and son with him, it essentially brought my mother and him onto the same page. His suicide and the tragedies that surrounded his suicide brought back all the insane misunderstandings surrounding my mother's death.

The painting of realism the counselor canvassed for me slowed the momentum of the crazed thoughts running through my mind that day. I was finally able to understand why Chris Benoit's death and that of his family caused so much turmoil in my head. He had become a hero, someone I looked up to, and in that, his death would affect me strongly; I just never imagined how strongly.

After a good night's rest on base that evening, I was able to drive home the next day. I've had several conversations with Marvin since then, always thanking him for saving my life that day. I don't think he realized just what he had done for me. On that day, Marvin had become a hero.

I often look back on June 25, 2007; that day was a tragedy in so many more ways than the media ever knew. No one can know the pain that the family members of Nancy and Daniel

Benoit experienced and continue to experience on a daily basis; however, I do think of them often and hope that they have been able to find some peace within the destruction. I do however know at least a little of the pain that Chris Benoit's family and close friends feel. These are individuals who will live the rest of their lives with the question of "why" waking them every morning. These are individuals who search for reasons that will never truly be understood even if they are found. The added pain that these individuals feel is that of knowing two innocent people lost their lives by the hands of a man whom they idolized and looked up to as a hero. These individuals, as with me, are never allowed again to speak outwardly of the great man we once knew or at least dreamed we could have known. The rest of the world sees him, understandably, as a monster. But those of us that knew Chris or followed the passion that made him what he was will always remember him as one of the best at what he did.

I will never condone the violence that was disseminated at the hands of Chris Benoit. But I, like too many others, will forever be shadowed by the way he died.

23

Too Much, Too Soon

🎵

From 2001 to 2005 I served as an instructor at the DoD Fire Academy at Goodfellow AFB, San Angelo, Texas. Through this job I gained a great respect for teaching the younger generation of firefighters to be the best they could possibly be.

In March of 2007 a message was sent over the Minot AFB communication waves announcing a job opening at the local Airmen Leadership School (ALS). ALS is a form of professional military education in which up-and-coming sergeants are taught the ins and outs of Air Force supervisory expectations. In this I saw an opportunity to grow as a military leader and build the new generation of supervisors at the same time. Additionally, stress and suicide were curriculum issues taught at ALS, and I figured I could bring personal insight to the presentation.

Because of my previous instructor experience, I was selected and spent the next five weeks in training at the Gunter Annex of Maxwell AFB. After completion, I began my on-the-job training. My previous four years of teaching was from a completely different format so it took me a while to grasp the style differential, but I'd like to think I had potential.

Week three with my first class arrived very quickly, and with no major hiccups. However, the day before I was set to teach the "stress and suicide" unit, an airman from the base killed himself. It just so happened that the victim's best friend and two other coworkers were in my class. Obviously, this shoved the stress meter precariously close to the top.

I did my best to prepare everyone for the next day's topic and assure them that no matter how difficult it might be, we would get through it. I'm not sure that I was trying to convince them or myself. But the next day dawned with anxiety continuing to mount. Simply put, I was dreading every minute of it. Tensions only worsened as I entered the classroom to find that I was being evaluated by one of my fellow instructors.

Starting my introduction, I followed my lesson plan for a full thirty seconds before my head started whirling. I found myself in a pressure cooker with all eyes locked on me. What was supposed to be a class wide discussion became a "survivors" tirade of the pain, depression, and devastation I felt after Mom's suicide. I lost complete control of all ethical instructional procedures as my portrayal of Mom's death was painted with obscene language injections and tension so thick it was suffocating. What was to be forty-five minutes evolved into an hour and a half, the majority of which I was later unable to recall. Every emotion I had bottled up, erupted violently and without restraint. Basically, I had a mental breakdown at the podium.

Immediately following class, of course, I was reprimanded for my actions. I knew I was out of line. Even though my boss assured me that everyone has a bad day, and that I could definitely bounce back from this, I knew it was too late; the damage had already been done.

The next two months were excruciating. I lost all confidence in my abilities as an instructor. My passion for inspiring others dissipated like morning dew. I tried everything I knew to bounce back, but it was useless. I hated going to work, afraid of being unable to restrain my emotions.

Dear Mom,

It's been a while since I've written you. I would say sorry, but what's the point?

I have been having a huge problem dealing with the depression as of late. It's been so bad that I'm about to lose a position that I've worked so hard to obtain. Every ounce of energy I've put into this thing was all for nothing. I just can't handle teaching the amount of material I need to teach and deal with missing you at the same time. I'm not myself anymore. Hell, I haven't been myself since you died. Every time I get three feet forward I get knocked five yards back. And the worst thing of all is that all the confidence I once had has been completely and totally obliterated. I'm lost ...

After three long months of misery and dread on the job I was graciously given the option of going back to the fire department. I left in good standing, but I knew if I didn't take this chance to leave with a clean slate, I would eventually be removed.

NOTE: I am a firm believer that if a horse bucks you off you get right back on. However, in situations like this, there's no problem starting back on a colt and working your way back up.

Looking back I realize I simply took on too much, too soon. Even though I took the ALS job with the best of intentions, the timing wasn't right. Even though I left with a clean slate and was welcomed back to the fire department with open arms, I still regret the way I left. Both lead instructors were outstanding mentors, and I could have gained a wealth of knowledge and expertise from them had I been able to tackle the job with a clear head.

NOTE: After your initial devastation wears off, do not try to take on too much too soon. Your emotional strength will come and go, and the backlash of pain may hit you when you least expect it. Step lightly into new endeavors; diving in head first may leave you in over your head, grasping for a lifeline.

24

What Definitely Didn't Help

B efore Mom's death I was an avid user of alcohol. After her death, I became an addict. Do I blame Mom's demise for my substance abuse problem? No. I had been a partier for years and definitely knew my way around a bar. But I had more control back then. After her death, alcohol felt more like a need than a want. Where it was once a temporary relief from the stressors of commonplace life, it slowly manifested into something much worse.

Treatment was a blessing in disguise; I just didn't know it at the time. It allowed me to speak and think my way through all the chaos, as well as concentrate on ridding myself of something I never really needed in the first place.

Immediately after completing my stint in treatment, I made a goal to stay sober for a year. It was rough going from time to time; nevertheless, I did achieve it. The problem was that after attaining that goal, I never set another. I didn't decide to stay clean or go another year, and with no more goals to shoot for, it was only a matter of weeks until I was popping a top again.

Depression, chased with additional depressants, yields a black hole; it's basically swimming in agony while thirsting on death. Alcohol is exactly that. I loved it and hated it all at the same time. I remember drinking a beer or a shot, all the while my subconscious saying "this is exactly what you don't need." When you repeatedly tell yourself all day that you're not going to drink, yet you eventually find yourself pulling into the nearest liquor store, you have a serious problem. My alcoholism went in spells. I'd be good for a few months, begin to feel like I could handle it again, start back, and within a matter of days be worse off than I was when I last quit.

In early 2009, we were transferred from Minot, North Dakota, to Okinawa, Japan. Like most addicts I figured a change of scenery would help me decrease the alcohol intake. Not a chance. Fleeing from addiction doesn't lessen the thirst. It was only a matter of months before I was drowning in alcohol again.

I hated alcohol every time I was sober, but loved it while consuming it. Writing this book has been both healing and challenging. Recounting the sources of depression can sometimes pull me in a direction I can't afford to go. Depression makes me thirsty; drinking makes me depressed … it's a revolving door. Eventually, I realized I had to stop the drinking forever or lose everything I have worked so hard to achieve.

NOTE: My intention is not to tell you what to do; however, if there is one tidbit of knowledge you gain from my experiences, let it be that alcohol only makes things worse. The loss of a loved one is depressing enough; alcohol in addition can be devastating.

I now realize that the majority of pain and suffering I experienced was only enhanced by the effects of alcohol. Some people can drink and enjoy it without experiencing its negative effects. I'm not so lucky. But where I once felt regret, I no longer allow myself to. Each mistake I've made in my life has become a source of outreach I now use to help others. Alcoholism has simply become another tool in my arsenal.

25

Embracing the Insanity

𝓻

Peple have asked me about my tattoo which translates from Japanese Kanji to, "Insanity is a gift from God." No one ever seems to understand my appreciation for that quote. From childhood we learn that insanity is a bad thing and that "crazy people" are all cursed in one way or another. I once agreed with those ideas. But looking back on my life, I never was what you might call a "normal" person for normality always played itself out to be boring and dull. As stated before, I was more of a deep thinker; an innocent mind with sinister evaluations of life's outcomes. I always expected the worst from every situation. Then, if it became reality, I was prepared. But if the outcome was better, then it was like getting a gift: totally unexpected.

When Mom died, my complex mind quickly became a nightmare's playground. My romance with the gray area of thought and reasoning turned into a battlefield where death and life fought for what was left of my whimpering existence. Fortunately, I won the battle by realizing that death was my life's calling. I slowly began to find tranquility inside of insanity's prison ... turning my suffering into a quest to end others' suffering. Fighting my personal war against suicide was exhausting, both mentally and physically. So instead of curing my insanity, I embraced it. I hated what Mom's suicide did to me, but I realized it was now part of me. All the anger, fear, pain, and resentment I dealt with since her death would now be the fuel to ignite my passion for saving others.

Mom's death was an absolute nightmare; an all-encompassing insanity. But if I can use that nightmare to ensure others would not have to suffer, then it was worth it. So, ironically, I regained my life by embracing my insanity. Therefore, I concede that, "Insanity is a gift from God."

NOTE: In our weakness, God's power is perfected.

26

Getting the Family Back

🖋

Excerpt from May 26th, 2010

It took four years and some change, but I believe I'm finally beginning to get my family back. Since Mom's death, my father has not been anything like the one I knew as a child. He has busied himself with filling voids and protecting what wasn't there anymore rather than being concerned with those who had suffered the pain along with him. He has been more concerned with burying the past rather than rebuilding the future. I have spent the past two days in Bryan trying to get as much one-on-one time as I could possibly muster. I was extremely surprised to find that Dad had returned to the man I remembered. He was the one that initially opened our first discussion talking about Mom and the way he had mishandled the time after her death. These past two days have been the most uplifting and beneficial that I have spent with him since she passed.

No words can describe how much destruction Mom's death has had on the men of this family. Ever since that terrible moment, I've longed for the day all of us would break out of our mindless prisons to address the situation together, head on. Scotty was so defensive and hateful toward the version of Dad that we saw after her death that he literally re-organized his family as being just he, Megan, and their children only. Yes, he still treated me as a brother, but only when it was convenient for him. He was not the same brother I grew up with. But now, it finally seems like he's starting to release the protective shield he's held on to so intensely. He's once again turning back to the big brother I've always loved and tried to emulate.

Scotty, Dad, and I will never be the same as we were before she died, understandably. But at least it appears we are all trying to mend the fences and rebuild for the future.

Talking to Dad these past two days has been incredible. His protective cocoon is finally beginning to crack. What is going to be the hardest for Dad is opening himself up to the emotions and pain he has not allowed himself to feel. I hate knowing some of the issues he's about to face, but I also know that he did it to himself. He refused to take the downtime we begged him to take. Instead, he rushed back in to life too quickly. He never truly took the time to mourn Mom's loss.

To a point, I can understand his hurry. After thirty-five years of marriage to my best friend, I would probably do the exact same thing. How do you go from seeing the same face smiling at you through the glass door everyday you get home from work to never having that again? People were so quick to judge him for his actions, but did anyone try to look at the situation from his shoes? No, not even his own sons.

I saw sorrow in Dad's eyes as he talked about the past few years. I could see the unhappiness draped across his face. I can't say he regretted his decision to marry Vickie; he was just letting go of the numbness that had been his protection. It's taken him four years to let it go, and now he's finally grieving.

Dad had always talked about retiring and moving to the river; this was the first time he'd mentioned it since June of '06. But this time his reasons were disturbing. Dad has become increasingly discontented with the rat race of life and the stupid things people make into issues. He told me how sick and tired he was of other people's idiocy, and how much he wants to relocate to the simplicity of river life. But I can't help but wonder if there's more to it. Dad is finally beginning to feel the pain of Mom's loss, and I'm wondering if he might be afraid of being subject to a loss like that again. The river is his sanctuary, his place of Zen, and in my mind, the one place he feels impervious to pain.

Dad has dealt with a lot, even as a child ... from losing both parents within a month's time to being raised by people who didn't understand him. He had developed a tough outer shell. With Mom's death, I think Dad simply dismissed it, just as he had to with so many other hardships. But the pain has made a crack in that shell, and it's not going to be as easy to dismiss this time. Mom left him as the only parent, and through his quest to try and reinvent what's gone, he almost alienated both his sons.

Dad apologized to me and told me he was sorry for anything he may have done during this four-year period to upset me. He told me there was nothing more important to him than his sons, and that he was going to try to be the father we needed him to be. He also said he was going to try and make amends with Scotty and that we would get through the rest of whatever was to come in life, together.

It's taken four years for all of us to finally start meeting again on level ground. In my mind, it's about damn time.

It took years, but finally, we became a family again. It wasn't easy; of course, nothing worth having ever is. We still miss Mom, but our lives must continue even though she chose not to.

Excerpt from 15 Jan 2012

I am currently sitting inside a church with my birth family: my dad and brother, and their families. It is nothing short of a miracle to see where we are now from where we once were. Just five years ago, this scenario was only a figment of my imagination. Where once a vested battle raged, now only peace and harmony remain. None of us chose the path which was placed before us, but through time and patience we have become a family once again. She who is no longer with us is missed, yet we refuse to contemplate the "whys and what fors" any longer. We simply accept, pray, and move on with the purpose of why God has brought us together again.

I'm sure that the struggles are far from over. There will still come days that the only word we can mouth is "Why?"

But at least now I know that we will muster the courage and strength to face such struggles together as a family. Separations have been bridged; fences have been mended. Time, patience and love are great healers.

27

Almost Gone

Peace .....it is absent in my presence. No matter how much I plead for it, it merely mocks me, dodging my reach.

God, hear me. I must find peace at least for one hour of one day. I'm nearing the point of no return. I'm almost to where I can no longer deal with the lies, deceit, and madness in my head anymore.

Saturday, 10 August, 2010, was my extra day off from work, but I had scheduled a meeting with my airmen to handle some needed business. Arriving home, I felt extremely tense and ill at ease, though why, I was unsure. I decided to let Natalie sleep in and do a little cleaning around the house.

The quiet didn't last long as the kids soon made their way down stairs. I fixed them a quick breakfast and returned to my chores. Once they finished eating, the normal morning ritual began of watching cartoons and destroying anything in their path. Jostacia, bless her heart, kept messing up everything as fast as I cleaned up, and it started to irritate me. My irritation escalated quickly then exploded when, flipping up her blanket, Joi's Pop-tart pieces scattered all over the living room. I reacted without thinking. I didn't yell ... I screamed at her loud enough to make both kids hide under the pillows.

Whatever was bothering me caused me to lash out at the two most undeserving individuals in the world. I tried my best to calm them down. Then I went upstairs and told Natalie I had simply "snapped" and I had to get out of the house. Concerned, she tried to understand and agreed it would be best if I took a drive to calm down.

I drove off base toward the coast line, knowing that the fresh ocean air and scenery has always rejuvenated and uplifted me. My bitter thoughts and growling stomach were playing games with my head, so I stopped in at one of my favorite spots to grab a bite to eat. Placing my order, I took a seat and grabbed a pen and paper to jot down my thoughts. Immediately, my hand went ballistic scribbling down every thought besieging my mind. As soon as I finished, I signed my name at the bottom. Reviewing my rantings, I was blown away to realize what I had penned was not any common synopsis but a suicide note.

What happens when you wake in the morning and care nothing about being the person you are anymore?

What happens when the face in the mirror is no longer recognizable?

What happens when the beauty of your children is tainted by the anger you have for yourself?

What happens when your brain can't stop screaming?

What happens when you work your fingers to the bone yet realize that your devotion means nothing to the slave drivers you serve?

What happens when you fight to free yourself from the insanity which killed a loved one then realize that you're in love with such insanity?

What happens when your love for life can't measure up to the desire you have for death?

What happens when the only thing that brings a smile to your face is the thought of everyone forgetting you exist?

What happens when love just isn't enough?

What happens when you simply don't care anymore?

What happens? You do this.

Nelson Thomas

I was losing my grip. I had not consciously thought of suicide, but obviously my subconscious had. I had to leave. I was running, though I had no clue from what or where I was going.

Inevitably, I ended up at the only place of Zen I ever identified by my own eyes; Taguchi Beach. Somewhere between the restaurant and the beach, I had talked with Natalie and other friends over a dozen times, apologizing for any pain I had caused them. They knew I was very distraught. At some point, I confided to my close friend that I was going to my place of Zen, which is what pointed my wife to my location.

When I arrived at Taguchi Beach I immediately went to my spot, the only spot I've ever found peace. I laid there on the beach for what felt like hours, trying to regain some resemblance of sanity; but it continued to evade me. I fought an embittered battle to dispel thoughts that kept hammering my head, "load yourself down with rocks and take a swim." I laid there crying, knowing that if something didn't give, I would soon be wherever Mom had gone.

Finally, after battling the demons for as long as I could with no relief to be found I began to search for the heaviest rocks I could find. It was at that moment that I heard Natalie's panic-stricken voice calling my name. In disbelief, I looked to the top of the reef to see her and my Operations Chief from the Fire Station rushing toward me.

Needless to say, If Natalie hadn't shown up when she did, this book would have never been finished. What followed was a period of indescribable mental anguish like none other. But through this closest encounter with death, I found out exactly what was going through Mom's head when she pulled that trigger. She wanted relief and calm from whatever demons were haunting her.

I can't say that it was exactly the same, but to a point I saw, felt, and experienced firsthand what my mother did in her final minutes of life. I hate that I scared Natalie and all around me like that, but in some ways, I am almost grateful it happened. It allowed me to see into a world that Mom saw. It is a world I hope to never encounter again.

After much needed therapy with an exceptional counselor, I now understand what almost killed me. I had been spending almost every waking minute available pouring my heart and soul into this book. I was recreating the pain and suffering from Mom's death so intensely, in the hope that I could help others in some way, that I failed to take care of myself. I had failed to identify that my alcohol intake had increased drastically and my sleep-filled-nights had decreased nearly as much. In that, I almost let Mom's death and my stupidity kill me.

After that, I walked away from writing for almost six months. Part of me was afraid to pick it up again; afraid that I might not survive the next time. In fact, at one point I decided it was over; I'd never come back to it again. But then I remembered that to me, quitting is much the same as being dead. I don't quit.

Returning to writing would not be easy. Here I was trying to save others from what had claimed my mother and yet I almost let it take me with her. If I was ever going to finish the book I had a lot of things to work through. I hoped someday to find the strength to overcome the fear and begin again.

28

The Awakening

Wednesday, 1 December 2010

The day started just like every other morning. Jostacia woke up her usual self … very moody and bossy. At one point, she copped an attitude with me. As she walked away, I noticed a slight limp. Natalie and I checked it out but couldn't detect anything, so we sent her on to daycare. But after school her limping was noticeably worse and now she was complaining of pain as well.

We took Joi to the emergency room late Wednesday night; X-rays revealed nothing. Still limping, we took Joi home with the usual round of antibiotics, assured from doctors that it was nothing to worry about.

But by Friday, we knew there was a definite problem. Joi was basically bedridden, and her complaints of pain had become persistent crying. Her right lower leg was now swollen and felt hot to the touch.

Natalie took her early that morning to the pediatric clinic at Camp Lester Naval Hospital on Okinawa for further evaluation. Around 11:30 Natalie called me and told me to get to the hospital immediately; that they were about to "put Joi under" to do some tests.

I drove like a mad man; I could not get there fast enough. My baby, my precious three year old daughter, was suffering with an unexplainable illness. I was beyond the point of terrified.

Arriving at the hospital, I had a mere fifteen minutes to see Joi and get caught up to speed on the latest before they whisked her away for an MRI. I cannot explain the helpless anguish I felt when that door closed, separating me from my baby girl. I stood at the door five minutes, pondering what was next if this scenario ended badly. I reflected on my actions since her birth. Had I been a good father? Had I told her enough just how much I loved her? It was a wakeup call.

Within two hours, Joi was in surgery for an infection in her lower leg between the bone and muscle. Doctors said we caught it early enough before any real damage occurred, though they had no clue what caused it. The true facts behind it remain a mystery today.

Jostacia spent the next five days in the hospital battling the infection. It was rough going at times, but today she bears only a scar. It was a horrific ordeal for her mother and me, but I now see it was divine intervention, an essential part of God's plan. How?

While Joi was in surgery, Natalie and I talked about our fears and desires if everything came out alright. Natalie pointed out that our priorities as a family had been significantly distorted and were much in need of a makeover. She also said it was time for us to start looking for a church again. Begrudgingly, I agreed. Though my past experiences with church congregations had been conflicting at best, this was no longer just about me or my issues with people as representatives of God's church. It was now about what was needed for my children, for my wife, and for our future as a family.

So Natalie and I stuck to our word and attended the "contemporary service" at Chapel One on Kadena AB the following Sunday after Joi's release. It was the first in what was expected to be a long road to find the one church where we all felt comfortable.

EXPLANATION: Natalie and I had previously attempted to find a church in which we could both feel comfortable with no success. Our religious upbringing was entirely different … Natalie's being very liberal, mine extremely conservative. I was willing to compromise on some things, but not abandon my basic beliefs and principles. So, needless to say, we encountered many obstacles in finding a place of worship that fit both of our expectations and needs.

So on this, our first visit to the chapel, we were pleasantly surprised with the progression of the services. But it was the delivery of the message that told us both that we were exactly where we needed to be.

Chaplin Humphrey is what I would describe as a "cute" individual … not at all what I expected, he was small all around in stature yet huge in inspirational delivery. I was hoping for a good, well-rounded message. What I got was a proverbial harpoon through the chest. To say he knocked one out of the park doesn't even cover it.

I am a note taker and I will let you know that I almost broke my fingers off as I scribbled his thoughts on to the page. The following is the majority of his main points along with my ideas which were spurred from those:

1) *"You being here today is part of God's plan."*
2) *"Your past week, no matter how productive or tragic it was is part of God's plan."*
3) *"Your overall past, no matter how bitter it has left you is part of God's plan."*

(All three of these statements were presented within the first minute of the lesson.)

Me—How can what's happened in my life be part of God's plan?

4) *"God wants to save you from the bitterness of your past."*

Me—What causes my overall bitterness?

- *Mom's suicide*
- *Not knowing what I'm supposed to do with the grief*
- *Not knowing if anyone will listen if I take a stand against suicide*

5) *Main Point # 1- "God has engineered our lives to fit into his plan."*

a. *"A sprout out of a dead stump"*

Me—What's my "dead stump"?

- *Mom's suicide*
- *Not just losing her but the way that we lost her*
- *Letting go of the idea that Mom killing herself would lead her to Hell*
- *The fear of making a stand against a disease that is killing people by the thousands and not becoming a statistic myself*
- *The fear of failing*

Me—What are my sprouts?

- *Jostacia being born shortly after mom's death*
- *The fact that I have a wife who supports my every endeavor*
- *My son who tries to do everything just like his father*
- *The legacy which summons me*

- *Those that I know I can assist if I just put my actions to work*

6) *Main Point # 2— "God placed you in the family you've come from for a reason."*

Me—Why? What point would he have to place me here?

- *He knows something I don't*
- *He knows that I have the ability to reach others*
- *What am I not allowing to happen?*

  o *To use the gifts he gave me*
  o *To step away from the fear that blankets me*
  o *To change Mom's legacy as it stands*
  o *Am I concentrating too much on my own wants and fears?*

    ▪ *Yes!!! You've known that for the past year*

7) *Main Point #3—"Giant green arrows versus the decisions of everyday life."*

Me- WOW!!!!!!!!

- *This lesson alone is a giant green arrow*
- *How many arrows have to be pointed before I finally realize what I must do?*
- *I have seen so many arrows*

  o *I have attempted to follow yet keep getting set off pace due my overwhelming fear of failure*

8) *Main Point #4—"There are no barriers in God's plan, only opportunities to grow our faith."*

Me- I've created my own barriers.

-   *I've allowed so many things to come undone*
-   *I have to finally accept Mom's tragedy for what it truly is:*

    o *An opportunity to assist others going through the same situation as mine*

    o *An opportunity to reach those hurting and considering suicide as an option before it is too late*

As I sat there, frantically writing, I began to realize that all of this pain we had endured over the past four years and eight months culminated in exactly what God had willed to happen. My battles with Him and confusion in the idea that He would never put more on a person than they could handle was not pointed at Mom, but at me.

As I look back I realize something I never allowed myself to see. Mom's sacrifice has enabled me to reach others in ways that she couldn't by herself.

All my life, I have believed that everything happens for a reason, an overall purpose. I immediately dismissed that idea as soon as Mom killed herself because no one at that time could have ever made me visualize a purpose to it. Now; however, I can literally see the map laid out in front of me. Mom died so that others may not suffer as much; so that a son, who never understood his purpose, could paint the truth behind what hell on earth is and assist others in overcoming theirs.

Joi's infection and surgery happened for a reason, and I don't need any worldly doctor's diagnosis to decipher it for me. It was part of God's plan. Mom's suicide and the nightmare that followed for almost five years is part of God's plan. My journey through that hell to embrace its insanity and come out whole again is part of God's plan.

NOTE: You reading this book, in whatever state your life is in, is all part of God's plan.

29

The Nightmare Continues

Just days away from what should have been the completion of this book in February of 2011, I experienced the loss of a dear friend and fellow firefighter. Derek Vincent Kozorosky was fatally injured in a vehicle-backing accident while at work at Kadena Air Base, Okinawa, Japan. I had the unfortunate duty to be the assistant chief in charge that day as we did everything we could to save our beloved friend. He was pronounced dead a few hours after the accident occurred.

Where life had finally returned to some sort of normality, Derek's death sent my world screaming out of control all over again. Though the accident was completely out of my hands, it took a huge toll on me. The job of an assistant chief is to ensure all personnel make it home alive; on that day, I failed. No matter how many times people assured me that his death wasn't my fault, I couldn't help but feel responsible.

From there, I crumbled into lifelessness. All the despair from Mom's loss returned tenfold, and I was immediately smothered by depression.

Accordingly, my alcoholism increased exponentially as I withered into a shell of my former self. Natalie did all she could to weather the storm as I breached insanity once again; consumed by the death of another so close. My body suffered new scars as I turned to violence during drunken stupors. From smashing my head into picture frames to punching concrete walls, I literally became an enraged, out of control monster. I did anything and everything negative to try to forget what could never be forgotten. Natalie found herself on the losing end of my desire for death as I would cry myself to sleep each night begging for her to kill me. She feared for my life yet hid her emotions, afraid of what might happen if she sought help for me.

Within five months after Derek's death, I officially hit rock bottom. All the lessons learned from Mom's loss were quickly forgotten with each tip of the bottle; an action that became habitual after his loss. Five years worth of restructuring was disintegrated and each day became a life and death struggle.

Natalie became extremely worried, not just for my own health but for leaving the kids with me as well. Where I would never before put Steven or Joi in harm's way, drinking and driving with them along for the ride became a continual occurrence. Often, Steven would be swept up in the emotions of my insanity as he would plead for me to calm down during frequent outbursts. In a matter of weeks, I became a father and husband none of them deserved to be around.

Life evolved into an all too familiar nightmare I prayed I would never relive.

30

The Final Straw

Life had finally hit its lowest point. I had done everything to self-destruct other than literally pulling the trigger myself. It was probably a great thing that we lived in Japan during this time and did not have easy access to a gun or I would have.

I eventually got to a point where I was doing absolutely nothing positive to simmer the overwhelming craziness in my head. I had sought counseling for persistent nightmares but even that had fallen by the wayside. I was allowing myself to be overworked. I was not eating healthy or taking care of myself physically. My drinking was at an all time high, and sleep was at a record low. I wasn't burning the candle from both ends; it was burnt with nothing left to give.

Throughout this entire book, you've seen my personal life wither into nothingness; all the while, my professional career still flourished. You see, I was always a very, "What does it look like from the outside" type of person. At work, I showed very little weakness when it counted. Meaning that I was always winning awards and doing things that made me look like the military poster child. Yet behind closed doors, especially those at home, I was a disaster waiting to happen.

You can be a beast at work, able to leap tall buildings in a single bound. But if your spiritual and family life is in shambles, eventually, something will give. And in true fashion, something did.

At fourteen years into my military career, and after having a spotless record, all of life's turmoil erupted at the one place I had never allowed to be desecrated: work. I will spare you the details, but in late July of 2011, I had what could only be described as the breakdown of breakdowns. From lashing out at higher ranking individuals and cussing in their face, to damaging personal property, my tirade exceeded epic proportions.

At first, I blamed everything and everyone other than myself. From stress to overwork, lack of sleep to lack of meds; just as long as the blame wasn't on me, I didn't care who it fell on. But after time, and once it all soaked in, I had no one to blame other than myself. I had allowed my life to unravel. I knew I was being overworked. I knew my stress level was at an all time high. Did I tell anyone? No. I trudged on with the burden, just as I always had. Yes, I had sought treatment for the nightmares, but I hadn't done anything about the drinking that was helping the nightmares and depression persist. Everyone searches for a hero during times of horror and distress. I didn't realize that I could have been my own saving grace during this time. I knew I was crumbling into oblivion, but I ignored all the warning signs in me that I am trained to identify in others. I should have been man enough to stop the train before it derailed; but I didn't. And I had no one else to blame for that failure but myself.

Thankfully, my previous record spoke volumes over this outburst and my career was spared, but not without severe consequences. I received max punishment for my actions. It was bad; but it could have been much worse.

Anyone reading this who worked with me prior to this event is probably not at all surprised with my outburst. I had become a monster; personally, professionally, mentally, and spiritually. And I will be the first to tell you that I deserved everything I got. But what bothers me the most is that my family life had been crumbling for years. My relationship with my wife was an up-and-down roller coaster. Though not physically, I had been mentally and spiritually abusive to not just my wife, but kids as well. My personal life was literally in shambles, but it took me getting in trouble at work for me to finally realize just how bad things had become. That's what disgusted me the most. What type of man allows his work life to stay intact while his personal life disintegrates in front of him? What type of husband and father places more importance on a trophy or a piece of paper rather than on his own family? I try to not allow myself to regret my past, but this fact was the hardest to forgive myself for.

I now praise God for allowing this situation to happen. Where in most cases, such reprimand buries a career forever, this changed my entire life. It helped me reprioritize everything: placing what's most important in its rightful place. I still work hard and am extremely proud of my career. But now, I ensure that my spiritual, mental, and physical health is well intact far before I contend with work issues. I have found that with a solidified foundation built and structured solely on God, all other responsibilities fall accordingly into place.

NOTE: I feel it's important to note that my leadership could have easily written me off after this situation. My actions were less than appropriate, and I could have easily lost my career due to such an outburst. Instead, my leaders used this opportunity to not only rehabilitate me but others who worked with me. They had to hold me accountable; no issue there. However, they also used this experience to ensure that the work force as a whole was being properly attended to. We had all suffered from Derek's loss, and my incident only proved that additional counseling and repair was necessary. From calling in crisis counseling teams to individual, one-on-one mentorship, my leadership did everything necessary to ensure our mental needs were met.

Additionally, I will say that it takes a great person to be on the receiving end of an outburst like mine, yet continue to be a friend and supporter of the deliverer. This individual could have turned his back on me, but he didn't. He remained a dear friend, and I have gained an immeasurable amount of respect for him because of it.

31

Purpose ... Found

From the book entitled *Bedside Blessings* by Charles R. Swindoll:

August 7

Every individual has a purpose for living—everyone of us. No one God brings to life on this earth is insignificant. The tragedy of all tragedies is that we should live and die having never found that purpose, that special, God-ordained reason for serving our generation. You have, like no other person on this planet, particular contributions that you are to make to this generation. They may not be as great as your dreams, or they might be far beyond your expectations; but whatever they are, you are to find them and carry them out.

There comes a point in most people's lives that the trivial pursuits, which once seemed so important lose their luster, such as the grand illusions of childhood where every boy dreamt of being a super hero and girls fanaticized of being whisked away by her own prince charming on a valiant white steed. Very few ever truly get all that they dream of, and many of us are left to deal with whatever reality brings our way. But what about those who are forced to deal with personal tragedy and horror? What about those certain individuals who always seem to smack face-first into fear yet somehow yield triumph over tragedy? It's these individuals who through suffering and tribulation find their true calling and obtain a focused balance of direction and responsibility.

Take John Walsh, for instance. John Walsh is known for his anti-crime activism, which he became involved with following the murder of his son, Adam, in 1981. Prior to Adam's abduction, John was involved in building high-end luxury hotels. John's life and passion completely changed with the death of his son. Following the crime, the Walsh family founded the Adam Walsh Child Resource Center, which eventually merged with the National Center for Missing and Exploited Children, where John now serves on the Board of Directors. His and his wife's efforts eventually led to the creation of the *Missing Children Act of 1982* and the *Missing Children's Assistance Act of 1984*.

John Walsh is probably best known as the host of Fox's *America's Most Wanted*, which he launched in 1988. It was the longest-running crime reality show in Fox's history and contributed to the capture of more than 1,000 fugitives. Today, Walsh continues to testify before Congress and state legislatures on crime, missing children, and victims' rights issues.

There is no doubt that John Walsh would have never expected such a horrific tragedy to strike his family. And I don't think anyone alive would have blamed him if he had crawled in a hole and sank into bitter depression for the rest of his days. But he did the exact opposite. John Walsh took this tragedy and committed himself to ensuring others would not have to share the same experience. The positive impact of his actions can never be measured. From implementing legislative actions that increase the safety of kids everywhere to ensuring perpetrators accordingly pay for their crimes, John Walsh has and will continue to affect millions.

No one should ever have to contend with losing a family member to tragic events; but this is reality. There are no fairy tale endings in real life. People will suffer tragedy. But it's what they do in the wake of that tragedy that proves their worth. Will we fold under pressure or will we rise above it all to find an overall purpose for this crazy life? As stated before, I always believed that everything happens for a reason. But once a tragic event takes place such as losing a parent to suicide or a son to child abduction, it's extremely difficult to idealize reason from horror. In my case, as with most, eventually time suppressed those initial emotions, and I found myself searching for purpose once again.

1 Peter 5:10 says that after you have suffered for a little while, the God of all grace, who called you to His eternal glory in Christ, will Himself perfect, confirm, strengthen and establish you.

Once the shock and awe wore off from each tragic event I experienced, I too wanted to find a reason for it all; a purpose for the pain. I grew so tired of blaming God and focusing on all the negative things. I yearned for logic and rationale. Overtime, as the confusion faded, I found that one thing had continued through all my former hopelessness: my writings. As I stated in the beginning, I have been obsessed with putting pen to paper for years. Scribbling and jotting down all the weirdness in my head. I've always found the practice of writing my thoughts and ideas on paper to be quite liberating. But I've normally written for my own enjoyment, not with the intentions of having others read it.

It wasn't until three years after Mom's death that I considered turning all of my ramblings into a book. But my considerations were only half-hearted anyway because I had no faith in myself to ever be able to complete such a task.

I try to be a fairly sharp individual when it comes to my career, but let's just say that I was a few hundred people back from winning the valedictorian honor from my high school. How was a guy who successfully types a whopping eighteen words per minute and has a chicken scratch worse than a doctor believe that he would ever be able to write a book?

The other debilitating factor of it was that to write such a book, I would have to regurgitate all the pain of my past in order to make it happen. It's not always easy to look back on the past. Initially I found that conjuring up all that pain only created more pain. Imagining my mother with a gun in her hand hurts me. Remembering the insanity, addiction, and depression which followed her suicide hurts me. Reliving the tragedy of Derek's accident and the continual bombardment of those images hurts me. But eventually I found that the more I pressed to help others, the more the pain subsided. I will never completely forget, but now those emotions fuel my passion to aid others during their darkest days.

My purpose was fairly easy to find. I've spent the past fifteen years being an Air Force Fire Fighter. In my opinion, there are very few other careers that embody the heart and passion to care for others as this. Being a firefighter and EMT trained me to put the needs of others well before my own. It also built a desire to impact others emotionally and spiritually as well as physically. So finding the reason was simple.

Where I experienced so many issues was in contending with my day-to-day life all the while trying to reach so many others who were themselves suffering. Each time, the deeper I'd got the more my demons and addictions would latch on for the ride. The more I relived each experience, the more my head would get discombobulated and overwhelmed. I soon found that my empty core didn't yield much protection from the "lies, deceit, and madness in my head."

But all the years of mental illness, heartache, and turmoil

came face to face with "purpose" and meaning during the Thanksgiving weekend of 2011. As I stated in the very first chapter, one major affirmation I had failed to establish in my early years was a solidified relationship with God; each chapter since has verified that my existence has sunk further and further without that divine foundation.

The Thanksgiving weekend of 2011 had arrived finding me in a deep despair following the recent loss of Derek and my professional downfall at work. I was trying desperately to keep my head above water, but the built-up depression and anxiety had cut me deeply, and I was floundering at best. I was still wallowing in my egotistical pity, blaming everyone else but me for my then-current work issues. Having had met Derek's parents in March, I kept visualizing what they were experiencing with this being their first major holiday without their son. This visualization, mixed with years' worth of pain and further rage due to my work situation left me in more than just a foul mood. I found very little to give thanks for at that time in my life and simply wanted the weekend to pass by with me unharmed.

Expecting the large amount of grief I would probably contend with that weekend, I had told Natalie that I was not drinking at all, looking to avoid the influx of any additional depression. But addiction came calling stronger than ever, and I quickly found myself three sheets to the wind the entire four-day period. Again, I knew it was the last thing I needed; I simply couldn't stop.

But an amazing revelation evolved that following Sunday that can only be defined as an act of God. Hung-over and extremely dehydrated, I spent the majority of the morning on the couch attempting to awaken what little energy I had left. I had always heard that God worked in mysterious ways; this next part simply proves that notion. Natalie, apparently disgusted by my inebriated state, stared down at me from across the room. "So, I guess you don't feel like doing anything again today?" she asked. And then "It" happened. I looked at her and saw an all too familiar look of disappointment on her face. Bam!!! I don't know exactly why God chose that moment to grab hold of my life, but it happened in that exact moment. That last look of disappointment is all it took to awaken me like never before. I immediately decided that I was done with alcohol. There was no question in my mind as to how; it was done. I spent the rest of that day prioritizing everything in my life. From what I had taken for granted to the one being I had shunned all together, everything divinely started to fall into place.

The very next day I willingly checked myself into substance abuse treatment and told my leadership that I had to get help for everything that had gone wrong in my life. I lined up appointments from Mental Health to the Chaplain's Office in order to ensure all aspects of my treatment were covered.

From there, God began to trickle hints of purpose ever so subtlety into my growing sense of peace. The further away from alcohol I got, the closer my bond with Him grew. Fears which had haunted me, causing me to cling to the bottle, began to disappear. Hope in its purest form sweltered as the all-too-familiar depressant cloud finally dissipated. Reality began to set in, and I started to visualize where I had originally gone wrong. It wasn't the pain and despair after the tragic losses or the dependency on a liquid that nearly took my life. My wrong turn began when I walked away from God as a teen. The deeper my relationship grew with God the more I realized that a great deal of this sorrow and pain could have been avoided if I had simply focused my life on Him rather than on myself.

With each passing day I could feel the warmth of God's promise on my heart. He began to show me things so evident that I had never realized due to the encompassing haze delivered from each tip of the bottle. The true beauty of life unfolded in front of me, and I clung to each demonstration of its magnificence.

I quickly began to saturate each moment of my life with a better understanding of God. I fled from focusing on the actions of others in association with God and accordingly established this new relationship solely on Him. I sought knowledge from the Word and constructed my understanding and my principles from what I read. While I did seek counsel from biblical mentors, I ensured that my faith was built on God alone.

In my pursuit to build a complete bond with God, I took to listening quite frequently to Joyce Meyer podcasts I downloaded to my computer. From those, one particular topic became my favorite; it's entitled, "It's Time to Stop Running." There comes a part in this lesson where Joyce mentions the word *broken*. She stated, "Brokenness is not an ugly frightening word. To be broken in the right places is the most beautiful thing that could ever happen to you." She went further to describe a point in her life where she was badly hurt by the actions of those around her and that it was one of the best things that had ever happened to her. And then she said the one thing that has stuck with me ever since. She declared in a bold voice that, "everything don't have to feel good to be God."

I so emphatically agree with this statement. There have been times in my life when pain was all I felt. But now that the pain is past and I have accepted the purpose God created for me, I can verify that everything indeed does not have to feel good to be from God. There was no peaceful easy feeling during the gradual spiral which left me broken. But once I was there; totally broken and destitute, God took no time to start recreating and renewing me to be the person, the instrument, he needed me to be.

My brokenness came over time and through different experiences. Everything I had clung to for so long and found importance in showed its true face and ultimately left me brokenhearted. I spent years trying to find the one situation which makes me truly happy. I tried alcohol, with a backwards effect. I thought engulfing myself in my work to gain awards would do it, again, nothing. Finally, I figured if I simply spent my life making everyone else around me happy, I would be as well. Unfortunately, I learned the majority of the world is ungrateful. So after all that it came to a simple answer that my parents tried to teach me from the very beginning. To be truly happy I now put God first, my family second, ensure my personal limitations are identified and prayed for and allow God to handle the rest.

"If through a broken heart God can bring His purposes to pass in the world, then thank Him for breaking your heart."

— Oswald Chambers

A statement I posted to Face Book:

I was approached by someone yesterday who asked me what had happened to me. When I inquired to their meaning, they said that my FB posts had gotten boring, being that all I ever talk about anymore is God, finding my purpose in life, and loving my family. He said I was more entertaining when I complained about work all the time. After considering his comments, I've come to this conclusion. For years I always worried about being cool in other people's eyes. I lessened myself to their expectations of what I should be rather than building myself for what God wanted of me to be. Anger, rage, and frustration ruled, leaving me with no idea of the true meaning of peace. I eventually got to a place in life where all I wanted was death. But then, in His divine timing,

God wiped away all those things and revealed to me the importance of His direction versus my own. My passion turned to His, and each day since has been filled with loving and serving Him, walking in His purpose for my life, and loving the amazing family He has blessed me with. If doing these things makes me "uncool" in the eyes of the world, so be it because I am no longer concerned with entertaining the world. My sole purpose is in Him. Anger, rage and frustration no longer have a place in my life, and I wouldn't ask for it to be any other way. I pray for those who search for acceptance from the world, for the world can't even accept itself. Harmony in God is my peace and I pray that they might find their way in Him as well.

I once wished I had experienced a different and easier past. I now praise God for entrusting me with such knowledge and for crafting me into the instrument I am for him today. Through He who gives me strength, I now use my past to aid others into finding their future.

32

God's Subtle Reminders

Among all the hardships I experienced, there were occasional inserts of brilliance that presented proof of better days to come. Some of these experiences were simple spur-of-the-moment events where others were entities that had been there all along, but I was either too proud or bull-headed to realize it. What I didn't see then, I now identify as God's subtle reminders of His presence in my life.

On August 13th, 2010, just one month after my close call with death, I had an experience that reminded me that life, no matter how much we may wish otherwise, continues. It started as a normal day at the fire station, but it soon became so much more. I was the crew chief on the primary response engine and shortly after shift change we were dispatched to a report of a woman in labor. Hearing this, I knew it would most certainly be an interesting day.

NOTE: One of the greatest experiences of my life occurred on August 1, 2003. On this day, I had the amazing opportunity to help deliver my son, Steven. Having had this experience and being a certified EMT since 2006, I was up to the challenge.

The emergency played itself out in a very interesting

way, but it brought with it a new baby girl into the world. As I acknowledged earlier, I truly do believe that things happen for a reason, and this experience was no different.

With all the pain and strife I was still going through, delivering this baby gave me a whole new perspective on life. I've learned that one must be willing to take the good with the bad; to accept the things which cannot be changed and change the things that can. Years prior to this experience had been filled with a great deal of loss and despair. However, on this day, life, in its purest and most perfect form reminded me there were still things worth living for. It reminded me that I could still contribute something positive. It became the starting point to bring about the change I needed.

Less subtle but definitely something I view as a blessing from God is my career. Being an Air Force Firefighter is a huge part of what makes me who I am and has definitely simplified the process of seeing my purpose in helping others. This career has given me a since of pride I can never truly explain in words.

When I originally entered the Air Force I expected it to be a simple four-year hiatus from the outside world. But the more time I served, the more I began to love the military life. I'm not trying to make this sound like a recruiting scheme, but it truly has been more of an adventure rather than a simple job. Through it, I have witnessed both the creation of life and the coming of death. I've assisted people in their darkest hour and smiled with them in their happiest of moments. It's where I met my beautiful bride and where we raised our children. It's where I gained a true understanding of the terms, "commitment" and "sacrifice." It was a part of me when I lost my mother and quickly became the only source of meaning and purpose I found during my decimated existence. Though not always easy, it has solidified my desire to serve others and become a catalyst through which I can help and heal others.

By the grace of God, for the past ten years there has been one constant in my life during times of tragedy and turmoil: one solid entity that never lost faith in me, and that is my wife, Natalie.

Since the day we met, Natalie has been my biggest supporter, even during the worst of times.

I've always believed the age old adage that "behind every good man is a great woman." Now, I don't know exactly how "good" of a man I am, but I can testify that any good intent that has come out of me since she came in my life has definitely been inspired by the beauty and magnificence that is my wife. She is the foundation that keeps me grounded … well, as grounded as possible.

Throughout this book I've identified friends who have either assisted, saved my life, or both. But mark my words; I am still alive and somewhat sane today due to the love and support of Natalie Jostacia (Alexander) Thomas.

12 Dec 2011
Dear God,

I don't know if I've ever said this to you, but thank you for bringing Natalie in my life. What an amazingly wonderful woman she is. She is my love; my one true soulmate. She is my angel on earth. I pray that you continue to tear away this diseased shell of a man that she knows and allow me to become the husband she deserves. I ask that you take my life and

*use it for your will. Through this she will know love
beyond all understanding.
Amen*

In July of 2012, I was driving somewhere in Okinawa City with Steven and Joi. Obviously not in a total sense of emergency being that we were on an island and would eventually find our way, we were still lost from our desired destination. After driving furiously for twenty minutes without finding the location, I announced to the children that we were officially lost. Without skipping a beat, Steven looked up at me and confidently said, "I know exactly where we are, Dad." Dismissingly I asked, "And where would that be, Steven?" He responded directly, saying, "In God's hands." My frustration quickly dissipated as I felt a sheepish grin wrap across my face.

You have to love how much simplistic knowledge is possessed inside such an unknowing beholder.

I now realize that God was always with me, even during the worst of times. But it was the little things or ones I took for granted that now mean so much to me. In the midst of tragedy and turmoil we always focus on the negatives. But I challenge you through yours to search for the subtle little reminders God implants to remind you you're not alone.

Isaiah 43:18-19 reminds us to not call to mind the former things, or ponder things of the past. "Behold, I will do something new, now it will spring forth; will you not be aware of it? I will even make a roadway in the wilderness, rivers in the desert.

33

God Will Provide

On the evening of May 31, 2012, as I was getting ready for bed, I received a phone call from two men who had become very dear friends of mine. I had met John Kaczmar and Chris Kozora at church soon after my change of faith, and we quickly formed a bond like no other. On this particular night, John and Chris called to inform me that I had been on their minds and that they wanted to pray for me over the phone.

Before I go any further, I think it's necessary to explain something. Prior to my change of faith and during my countless attempts to stop drinking I found that sobriety always gained little fanfare from my friends. One in particular that I had been a tag team partier with consistently seemed to stop coming around as soon as the well ran dry. This always caused me a great deal of concern for one very important reason. Even though I come across as a fairly strong-willed and independent person, I have always needed to feel loved and accepted. Having support, whether positive or negative, from others was a must for me before I found strength in God. Therefore, losing my boozing buddies during periods of sobriety caused my loneliness to kick into over drive. So accordingly, when I finally gave up the bottle and put my life in God's hands, this friend reluctantly faded to the shadows. Due to this, I soon found that the only true and close support I was granted was from Natalie. That was until the day I was introduced to John and Chris. After sharing my testimony with them I quickly realized that God had provided the true friends I had needed all along.

So that brings me back to my original story. My two, divinely granted friends called to pray for me over a recent job opportunity that had revealed itself to me. As soon as I heard why they had called, I immediately felt a blanket of comfort encompass me, and I knew that God was in full control. So there I sat on the edge of my bed as these two friends and instruments of God pleaded for His will to lead my life. They prayed that whatever path was opened that it would be centered on praising Him.

As soon as we closed our conversation, I told Natalie what had happened. Soon after, I spent the remainder of the night crying and thanking God for both John and Chris.

If you ever find yourself anywhere near the broken road I traveled, you probably currently have or have had at least one person who has caused your heels to sink further in the muck of life. Know that if and when you start your ascent out of that dark place, this individual may try to tamper with your enlightenment. I tell you from personal experience that any friend who holds you back from accepting and following the path of God is anything but a friend. If you can assist this individual in establishing and building his or her own relationship with God, do not hesitate. But do not feel guilty for leaving someone to their affliction who's forcing you away from Him. God will provide the friends and support you need to liberate you from your past downfalls.

34

Faith by Fire

"One of the more significant things God will bring out of our grief and depression is an ability to walk constructively with others through theirs. In fact, one of the purposes of God's comfort is to equip us to comfort others."

—*David B. Biebel*

For all my years of questioning God for the pain and hardship I experienced, I now realize that these things had to transpire in order for me to be who I am today. God's purpose for me was forged by the loss and pain I experienced. Were these things easy to contend with? Absolutely not. Did I see a purpose for them as they came to me? No way. But now, after years of divinely granted wisdom and understanding, I've found my healing comes through providing assistance to others. A very dear mentor and friend, Chaplain Pat McCain, told me once that I have the ability to help people in ways he never can because of the experiences God has lead me through. My past almost killed me, but through God's grace, I have become a better man because of it; an instrument for His use.

Not long ago, I was approached by a long time friend of my mother's. This person didn't say much, but what she said meant more to me than I can confide. She simply said that she sees my mother in me and that every ounce of determination within me to reach others is a direct reflection of her. Those words made me feel as if Mom's arms were wrapped around me.

My family and I will experience further hardship; without a doubt. We could spend the rest of our lives blaming God, but for what purpose? All my years of anger and frustration granted me nothing but lost time. People will perish tragically. It's what we do in their absence that not only define us as children of God but also show that person's importance in our lives. We will never be able to bring those people back, but we can ensure that their spirit survives and endures through us.

For those currently experiencing their own version of hell on earth, let me say that everyone handles grief and pain in his or her own way. It cannot be dictated, nor will it follow a pattern so that we can know how long it will last or what to expect next. Some will exhibit anger while others bury their emotions. Some may pull their friends and family closer, while others may build walls that hold them at bay. Personalities may change for a short while or a lifetime.

I wish I could tell you the exact steps of the survival process, but even if I knew them, I wouldn't. Many people tried to decipher the madness in my head after Mom's suicide. No matter which direction I was pointed, it all came down to me doing what was best for me. Did I try the suggestions thrown my way? Absolutely! Desperation calls for further desperation. Eventually my relief from the insanity came by embracing it. Writing this book, putting pen to paper, and bleeding all the pain onto page after page was my way of coping. Justifying the death of a woman who died because love wasn't enough was my relief. Changing the legacy of a mother from senseless death back to saving lives is how I found peace again.

Life will continue if you don't give up on living it. There are better days to come, but its how you personally play each day out that determines the healing or hell that follows. You will hurt, understandably, but do not feel weak for this. Initially, pain is all you will know; comfort will seem only as fiction. And let no one tell you that you're wrong for relapsing on past emotions. Be cautious to use the advice of others; what has worked for them in a similar situation maybe the last thing that you need to do. Unfortunately, this is a journey that you must take on your own. Yes, others can assist you on your way, but recovery from a disaster must be found solely by each individual. The most important thing to remember is that you have to decide you want to heal before the healing process can begin. And once the process begins and better days start to show, don't be afraid to use your newly acquired knowledge to assist others during their time of need. From tragedy you can find success.

> *I still remember the pain and sadness like I experienced them yesterday. But that's all they are now; a memory. The best thing about memories is that you can choose to make better ones. I now choose to live no longer in the memory of a dead mother but to live for the beauty that surrounds me in my wife and children. I choose to walk with my head held high, basking in the fact that my purpose is no longer to run from death, but to embrace life. I smile my grandest smile in knowing that my destiny is not to take my own life but to save others through the strength God gave me.*

If you are the person suffering, barely clinging to what's left of life and considering silencing the madness in your head, I beg you to hold tightly to the truth that better days are yet to come. Do not be afraid to reach for those who can assist you. The more hell you keep bottled inside, the longer the nightmare will remain. Never feel weak in your thoughts or less of yourself. Everyone breaks from time to time. Everyone has their limits. Realize that life, no matter how dismal it may appear at times, is beautiful and well worth playing out.

The best advice I can give is simply to live; live each day one at a time. Reflect on the past just long enough to learn from its mistakes; do not dwell. Be optimistic for the future, yet never forget that the most important day of your life should be the one you're in right now.

For those who already have the blessing of knowing God, I pray that you continue on that path of righteousness and allow him to heal you and direct your future. Place your burdens and strife on the only being strong enough to carry them.

For those who do not know God or have not accepted His existence, I pray that you allow your heart to be open to the beauty of life and what life through Him can bring. I pray that you open your eyes to see the majesty that surrounds you daily. Give God the chance to do in your life what He has done in so many others. He can heal your pain and restore your strength, but you must be willing to trust in His almighty power. From someone who has seen the despair and destruction this world can bring, believe me when I say that God can raise you back out from the depths you're currently in. Allow Him to do that; allow Him to be your saving grace.

If you've been afraid of placing your life in God's hands because of what you've seen others who follow Him do, realize that they are not Him. Mankind will always make mistakes. Build your relationship on God and God alone, not on what your see others do in His name.

I now respond to emergencies and tribulations by praising God until they cease. No matter how hard I try to handle it, alone, I will fail. But with Him, all things are possible. Once I placed my faith, my belief and my life under his control, He gave me peace of mind.

28 July, 2012
Dear God,

This morning I woke up with an ambitious hunger to live, to smile, and to thank you for this life you've given me. Gone are the days that I begged for death. I can truly do all things through you who gives me strength. It is nothing short of a miracle to know where I once was to where we are now. I no longer walk this planet alone. You are my everything and my everything is you. Use your instrument thoroughly.

Nelson

ACKNOWLEDGMENTS

First and foremost, to God: "Oh ye of little faith." I never believed it possible to make so much prosperity from so much destruction. It wasn't until I realized that I could do all things through your guidance. Thank you for saving me from my demons.

To Dad: For every hug, pat on the back, or kick in the butt … thank you. I am the man I am today due to your love and leadership. If I can eventually be half the man and father you've been for us I will be one awesome person. I love you.

To Scotty and Megan: For showing me how to take it on the chin and keep swinging. Life has indeed been no picnic for the two of you, but together you have endured. Thank you for being great role models for mine and Natalie's relationship to follow.

To Vickie: For not giving up. You've supported us all even when we didn't support you back. Thank you for taking care of Dad when we couldn't.

To Natalie: For being my best friend, my soulmate, and my rock. I love you more than words can express.

To Steven and Joi: For being the only things able to put a smile on my face even through the darkest of times. Your mother and I are so very proud of both of you.

To the Kadena Chaplain's Ministry:

-Chaplain McCain: For making me understand what it truly means to love and cherish your wife. You are a beautiful representation for God on this earth and I can never thank you enough for your leadership as a Christian man.

-Chaplain Sellers: For giving me the opportunity to take that first step. You helped me identify God's purpose for my life.

-Chaplain Humphrey: For being a beacon of hope during the roughest trials of my life. Thank you for reminding me that I am still necessary.

To Greg and Teresa Alexander: For allowing me to be a bonehead for my first few years of marriage without killing me. Thank you for allowing me to be part of the family.

To Chris Kozora, John and Beth Kaczmar, Alecia Eastridge, Gregg Fells, Michael Wilkinson, Debbie Banta, and Chuck and Della Margelli for always supporting and encouraging me.

To Rob Martin, Monica McCain, Dan Gerome and Dani Cannon for taking time to read, edit, and encourage the completion of this book. I'm forever indebted to you.

To the publishing team at Xulon Press: For giving a guy with a message the means to reach others. Thank you for spreading God throughout the world. May this book be the first of many we complete together.

CPSIA information can be obtained at www.ICGtesting.com
Printed in the USA
BVOW031647120413

318042BV00001B/1/P